Quick Fixes With Mixes

Cakes
Cookies
Bars
Goodies

Great Tasting Desserts Made With Mixes

By
Lia Roessner Wilson

Published By
Cookbook Resources, L.L.C.
Highland Village, Texas

Quick Fixes
With Mixes

Cakes
Cookies
Bars
Goodies
Great Tasting Desserts Made With Mixes

1st Printing	August 2001
2nd Printing	June 2002
3rd Printing	September 2002
4th Printing	April 2003

Copyright © 2001
By Cookbook Resources, L.L.C., Highland Village, Texas.
All rights reserved.

ISBN 1-931294-03-8 (hardcover)
ISBN 1-931294-08-9 (papercover)
Library of Congress Number 2001099916

Front Cover Photo © 2000 John E. Kelly/Food Pix

Illustrations by Nancy Murphy Griffith

Designed, Published and Manufactured in the
United States of America by
Cookbook Resources, L.L.C.
541 Doubletree Drive
Highland Village, Texas 75077
Toll free 866-229-2665
www.cookbookresources.com

Flavors of Home™

Preserving
The Family Meal

INTRODUCTION

My experiences with cake mixes go way back. They've always come in handy when I've made decorated cakes because they were such a timesaver. In addition to being moist, they tasted good and made a great base for my decorating. Instead of spending time making a cake from scratch, I'd pop a cake in the oven made from a mix and then focus my time and energy on the icing and the decorations.

I then learned that they were useful not only as a "canvas" for my cake decorating, but also as a base for some really good desserts. I could add some ingredients to them and take a cake to a new level, like Cool and Fruity Lemon Cake on page 24 (this will be a hit for you in the summertime), or use them to make bar cookies, like Pecan Pie Bars on page 202—these bars are just like a pie, only easier to eat with your hands! Cake mixes can even be used to make cookies. You'll be amazed at how fast you can create a big batch of drop cookies using a mix and a few other ingredients.

In addition to **altering cake mixes to make cookies**, I figured that I could **do the same with a cookie mix**, so I started experimenting, mainly with sugar cookie mixes, to see what kinds of creations could be made. It's amazing what assortment of cookie tastes and styles can be made from a simple mix! I'm excited to be able to include some really cool cookie recipes in this book, such as Chocolate-Dipped Malted Milk Cookies, page 194, and a variety of sandwich cookies that reflect the holiday seasons, page 182. One of my all-time favorites, Ginger Jam Sandwich Cookies, page 180, has the wonderful flavor of ginger combined with jam in a pretty little cookie that you'd never guess was made from a sugar cookie mix. All of these can be made faster than you can say, "Please hand me that mix!"

I hope you have fun with all of the recipes included in this book. They are a cinch to make and I'm sure that there's going to be a favorite for everyone in your house. When you do find one that you particularly like, you can write it down in the handy Personal Index at the back of the book. Use the index to keep track of your favorite recipes by page, as well as write any special information you want to be sure to remember.

Happy baking!

CONTENTS

It's a Breeze 19

You'll find cakes of all kinds: including everything from a Bundt cake that requires no icing to a four-tiered torte complete with filling and frosting to sheet cakes that you simply bake, frost and then serve out of the same pan. With a few additional ingredients or an extra step or two, you can create good-looking and really tasty treats. It's all just a breeze, really!

Just Snap Your Fingers 149

You'll be amazed at the wide range of cookie styles and flavors you can create by using a cookie mix or cake mix as a base. The only thing more gratifying than making them is hearing the delighted squeals from family and friends who couldn't believe they were made from a mix! And they're all just a snap!

CONTENTS

BAKER'S TOOLS

(Fun Surprises You Can Give Yourself!)

You've got to have a spoon, a bowl and a cake pan, but there are a few other baking tools that aren't real necessities until you see how much fun and easier they make baking. Give yourself a special baking tool tomorrow and have a great time!

Cake pans
For stacked layer cakes, round pans are the best.

Bundt cake pan
One-pan cakes look great with or without icing.

Zesting plane
Make grating a breeze with this handy tool—cleanup is easier too.

Cake tester
Sometimes a toothpick just won't do.

Cake slicer
Get nice, flat tops
and perfectly even layers.

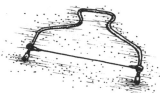

Silicone spatulas
Get every bit of that icing
or cake batter out of the bowl.

Skewer
Another great way to test for doneness—perfect
for testing the deep Bundt cakes.

Electric mixer
Once you try it,
you won't give it up.

Wire whisk
Bye, bye lumps.

Juicer
Quickly and cleanly gets
all the juice out of the fruit.

EASY TIPS

Following these few simple tips can help you bake better cakes—and make your life less stressful!

Turn Up the Heat

Don't forget to turn your oven to the required temperature before you begin mixing ingredients (that way, when you're ready to pop your cake in the oven, you don't have to wait for it to heat to the proper temperature).

Get Centered

Bake your cakes on the center rack of your oven. When using two pans (for layer cakes, for instance), position them in the middle of the oven, and don't let them touch each other or the sides of the oven.

Cool It

Cool your cake in the pan after removing it from the oven for about 10-15 minutes (unless the recipe specifies otherwise), before turning it out onto a cooling rack.

Don't Get Stuck

Grease and flour your pans—unless the recipe specifies otherwise. If you're not using an all-purpose baking spray for cake pans, then grease them first using a small piece of wax paper or plastic wrap and a tablespoon of shortening, and then dust lightly with flour (about a teaspoon or two). Shake the flour over the inside to coat, and then dump out. If you see any shiny spots, coat them and flour them before baking the cake.

Use cocoa to "flour" a pan for a chocolate cake to avoid the unsightly look of browned flour contrasted against the dark cake.

Test Your Cake for Doneness

There are a couple of methods for testing your cake toward the end of baking time to be sure it's completely baked before you pull it out of the oven.

The most reliable, I think, is using a cake tester (which can be a toothpick, bamboo skewer, or tool created for this purpose) inserted into the center of the cake.

If it comes out clean (or with only a few crumbs attached) your cake is finished. If it comes out with batter on it, you need to leave the cake in for a few minutes more and test again.

You can also lightly press the cake surface with your finger. If the cake springs back it's cooked.

Add "Zest" to Your Cakes
with Grated Fruit Rind

One of the best ways to add citrus flavor to your cakes is with grated fruit rind (like orange, lemon, or lime). Several recipes in this book call for "lemon zest" or "orange zest," and there are a couple of things to keep in mind when using this ingredient:

Only use colored part of the rind, not the pith (the white part), which can be bitter.

Grate the rind against the rough side of a grater over a piece of wax paper. When you're finished grating, you can gently lift the waxed paper, fold it slightly and shake the zest into your measuring tool.

Liquid Glazes

Several recipes in this book call for poking holes in a baked cake, over which you then pour a liquid glaze. The most effective method I've found for doing this (since many of the cakes that call for this technique are deep pans) is to use bamboo skewers, which you can easily find in the baking section or Asian foods section of your grocery store.

There are several reasons for this:

- They are just the right diameter for making holes large enough to absorb the icing, without damaging the surface of the cake.

- They also are easy on coated pans (you don't want to use a utensil that's going to gouge or scratch a non-stick surface).

- They are inexpensive and disposable, although if you want to, you can wash them and reuse.

- They are long enough to reach the center of a bundt cake where a toothpick won't reach.

TIMESAVERS

Using a mix as the basis for your dessert is the first step to saving time; however, there are some other things you can do to shave off a few minutes here or there, which may not sound like a lot of time, but added up can really make a difference.

Make liberal use of the microwave when it comes to softening ingredients like chocolate, butter or cream cheese.

Set the microwave cooking temperature on defrost for short cooking times (like 30 to 45 seconds at a time) and check each time to make sure that the ingredient is becoming soft without melting or cooking.

Grease and flour your pans! My favorite way to grease and flour a cake pan is to use an all-purpose baking spray designed for greasing pans. Not only is this fast, but it's less messy than using the traditional 2-step method of using shortening and flour.

If you're using a pan with decorative sides (like a Bundt pan), the spray also easily coats the indentations that are difficult to cover when coating by hand.

Make your cake ahead of time—If you know you're going to need or want a cake on a certain day, bake it a couple of days in advance and refrigerate or freeze it. (Cakes can be wrapped and frozen for up to three months in advance. Wrap them first in plastic wrap and then foil.)

When you're ready to use it, pull it out of the freezer, let it thaw, and then frost it.

Make your icing ahead of time and refrigerate it until you're ready to use it to keep it fresh. Just warm it to room temperature before using.

Most important of all–check your list of ingredients ahead of time to be sure you have everything you need!

I've made countless last-minute dashes to the store in the middle of baking a cake because I was missing an essential ingredient.

LOOK LIKE A PRO

It wasn't until I took a cake decorating course that I realized what kinds of tools and supplies were readily available for making homemade cakes look great. I was thrilled to find the cake slicer—no more miscalculated attempts to cut the domed top off a cake evenly with a knife. And the cake boxes were a real find. There's nothing worse than putting the finishing touches on a lovely cake you plan to take to a get together, to find that you then have no container to put it in for easy transport.

Your local hobby store carries a range of supplies, including cake boxes, cake boards, trim, pans and decorating tools. I keep a stash of cake boards on hand in several sizes—both round and rectangular. Although you can purchase decorative foil to cover the boards, I generally use aluminum foil. I wrap the board carefully, and then tape the foil down on the back. You can then put your cake directly on this, and if you want, then in a box. The boxes come flat and unassembled. They're wonderful for protecting your cake and making it easy to carry.

Cake Slicer
Slice your cakes neatly and easily with a cake slicer. I bought mine for about $3.00—a very worthwhile investment for getting trim, even layers.

Icing Spatula

An icing spatula makes icing a cake much easier!
You can get a really nice, smooth
finish not only on the top,
but also on the sides.

Cake Board

Often it's difficult to find a plate large and/or flat
enough to accommodate a cake, so a cake board
is a functional (disposable) solution.

Foil for Covering Board

Since your cake's appearance won't be
enhanced by the bare cardboard cake
board, you can cover it with
aluminum foil (which I frequently do)
for a nice surface. What looks even
better, however, is the gold foil
designed specifically for this
purpose. It looks very nice beneath
the cake, and is easy to apply to the
board. You simply cover the board and tape the
edges underneath.

Doily

If you don't want to use foil, or
even if you do, a lacy doily
peeking out from beneath your
cake can really be a dressy
finishing touch.

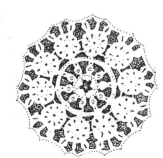

SPECIAL TOUCHES

*There are a few simple things that you can do on
your own to add some flair to your cakes and cookies.
They're much easier to do than you would think.*

Colored Sugar to Jazz Up Cakes and Cookies

You can easily make your own colored sugar to use
on cookies and cakes by adding a few drops of food
color to granulated sugar and then mixing well until
all the sugar is coated. Add 2 drops to ¼ cup of
sugar.

Candied Pecans

1 egg white
1 tablespoon water
½ cup packed brown sugar
2 cups pecan halves

Preheat oven to 300°. Grease a cookie sheet or
baking pan with a low rim. In medium bowl, beat egg
white and water until foamy. Add brown sugar; stir
until sugar dissolves. Stir in pecan halves until well
coated. Pour pecan mixture onto cookie sheet (some
of the sugar mixture will flow out from around the
pecans; thus the reason for the rimmed baking pan).

Bake until nuts are brown and crisp (about 25
minutes). Stir every 10 minutes or so and scoop the
sugar mixture onto pecans as you stir.

Remove from oven and stir to loosen nuts from
cookie sheet and separate from each other. Cool
completely and store in an airtight container at room
temperature. The candied nuts will keep for days if
you store them like this.

Chocolate Leaves

Few finishing touches look more stunning on a cake than leaves made out of chocolate. They're unbelievably easy to make and take nothing more than some chocolate, a cheap paintbrush (like the kind that comes with a water color set), and some non-toxic leaves from a bush or tree.

To make about 12 medium-sized leaves, first wash and thoroughly dry your leaves. Then take a 1 ounce square of chocolate and melt it. (I do this in the microwave; see tip in Timesavers section.) Dip your paintbrush into the chocolate, and holding the leaf by the stem (try to leave a stem on it for this purpose) paint a thick layer of chocolate on the back. Work in small sections, dipping your brush in the chocolate as necessary, until the entire back is coated. You can wait a few minutes and add a second coat. (You want the chocolate to be somewhat thick, so when you peel the leaf away it will be substantial enough to keep its form without breaking.)

Do this for as many leaves as you need, placing them on waxed paper to cool and harden. (I put them in the refrigerator to speed the process.)

Once cool, carefully peel the leaves away. (Try not to touch the chocolate with your hands, because their warmth will melt it. Use a toothpick to hold the chocolate as you peel the leaf.)

I've found that leaves with some flexibility work well. If they are too stiff, the chocolate breaks when you peel the leaf away. (Rose bush leaves work great. They are just the right size and keep their shape when coated.)

17

My Notes

It's A Breeze . . .

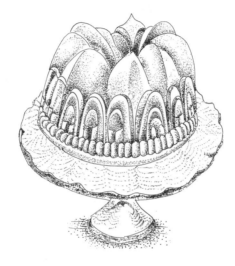

When it comes to baking, crafts or other hobbies, everything you make is created in steps. I'm always amazed that what appears to be difficult is really much easier than I thought if I just take it step by step.

Nothing here is difficult, so just take these cake recipes step by step and you will love the time you save and the rewards you earn.

And remember, it's all a breeze!

Sheet Cakes, Bundt Cakes, Layer Cakes, Tortes and Special Cakes

Sheet cakes, Bundt cakes, layer cakes, and tortes! You'll find cakes of all kinds in this section, including everything from a Bundt cake that requires no icing at all to a four-tiered torte complete with filling and frosting. There are even recipes for pastries created with cake mixes.

The versatility of the cake recipes located on the following pages makes it easy to find a cake for any occasion and for almost any pan. The multi-layered tortes provide the opportunity to go all-out and create a really stunning, towering cake with a little extra effort, as well as the flexibility to create a simple two-layered cake by leaving out the filling between the sliced layers.

Sheet cakes couldn't be any easier. Simply bake and frost, then serve out of the same pan. But don't be fooled by their simplicity; with a few additional ingredients or an extra step or two, you can create good-looking, delightfully tasty treats.

APPLESAUCE CAKE
WITH PRALINE TOPPING

½ cup butter or margarine
¼ cup heavy cream
1 cup packed brown sugar
1 ½ to 2 cups pecan halves
1 (18.25 ounce) yellow cake mix
1 cup apple sauce
3 eggs
½ cup milk
⅓ cup vegetable oil

Preheat oven to 325°. In medium saucepan, combine butter, cream and brown sugar. Cook over low heat, stirring occasionally, until butter is melted and sugar is dissolved.

Pour mixture into well-greased 9" x 13" baking pan. Sprinkle enough pecans evenly over to just cover the bottom of pan in a single layer.

In large bowl, combine cake mix, apple sauce, eggs, milk and oil. Beat on low speed to blend, then beat on medium speed for 2 to 3 minutes. Carefully pour batter evenly over pecan mixture. If necessary, very gently smooth top of batter to cover exposed pecan mixture.

Bake for 40 to 45 minutes, or until cake top springs back when lightly touched. Remove from oven and cool for 5 minutes. Turn cake out of pan onto serving tray, letting pan remain in place for 1 minute, then remove. If any praline topping sticks to inside of pan, just scrape it off and slap it back on the cake.

FLUFFY ORANGE CAKE

This chilly dessert is a refreshing way to cool down on a hot summer day. If you don't have time to freeze it, don't worry. You can simply make it in time to refrigerate and serve it cool. You may actually prefer it this way.

1 (3 ounce) package orange flavor gelatin
1 cup hot water
1 (18.25 ounce) yellow cake mix
4 eggs
⅔ cup vegetable oil
1 (8 ounce) package cream cheese, softened
1 (14 ounce) can sweetened condensed milk
⅓ cup fresh lemon juice
1 (12 ounce) container frozen whipped topping, thawed
2 (11 ounce) cans mandarin orange segments, drained and cut in half

Preheat oven to 350°. In small bowl, stir gelatin into hot water until dissolved. In large bowl, combine cake mix, eggs, vegetable oil and gelatin mixture. Beat on low speed to blend, then beat on medium for 2 minutes.

Pour batter into greased and floured 9" x 13" baking pan. Bake for 30 minutes, or until cake tester comes out clean. Remove cake from oven and cool.

(continued)

Prepare topping: In large bowl, blend cream cheese and condensed milk until smooth. Stir in lemon juice and mix well. Fold in whipped topping until blended. Fold in orange segments.

Pour mixture over cooled cake and smooth top over. Cover and freeze until 1 hour before serving.

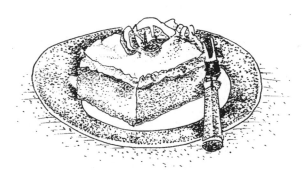

COOL AND FRUITY LEMON CAKE

You can use almost any fruit you like on this cake. Depending on what's in season, the fruit topping can be varied to suit your taste and what's in good supply at the time. Try exotic fruits like mangoes and star fruits for a unique taste experience and interesting presentation.

1 (18.25 ounce) yellow cake mix
3 eggs
⅓ cup vegetable oil
1 cup milk
¼ cup lemon juice
1 tablespoon lemon zest (grated lemon rind)

Preheat oven to 350°. In large bowl, combine cake mix, eggs, oil, milk, lemon juice and lemon zest. Beat on low speed to blend, then beat on medium for 2 to 3 minutes.

Pour batter into greased and floured 9" x 13" baking pan, and bake for 30 to 35 minutes, or until cake tester comes out clean.

While cake is hot from the oven, poke holes ½" apart over entire cake surface, and pour Lemon Glaze evenly over. Let cool, and smooth Whipped Topping over, and cover with fresh fruit. (Slice the fruit into ¼" thick slices and arrange attractively over whipped topping.)

(continued)

Lemon Glaze
2 cups powdered sugar
Juice from 2 medium lemons
Zest from 2 medium lemons
1 teaspoon orange extract

In medium bowl, combine sugar, lemon juice, lemon zest and orange extract. Stir until well blended.

Whipped Topping
1 (14 ounce) can sweetened condensed milk
⅓ cup fresh lemon juice
Zest of 1 lemon
4 ounces frozen whipped topping, thawed

In small bowl combine condensed milk, lemon juice and lemon zest. Blend well.

Fold in whipped topping.

Fruit
2 kiwis, sliced
1 banana, sliced
1 pint strawberries, sliced

I like to slice the fruit and arrange the kiwis in the middle, then fan strawberries out on either side, place a row of bananas, then a row of kiwis and end with strawberries for a starburst effect.

BANANA PINEAPPLE CAKE WITH BROILED COCONUT FROSTING

Delicious! This cake's light and delicate flavor is complemented nicely by the coconut frosting,
which isn't too sweet or rich.

1 (18.25 ounce) white cake mix
1 (8 ounce) can crushed pineapple with juice
½ cup milk
3 eggs
3 tablespoons vegetable oil
1 cup mashed bananas (about 2-3 medium bananas)

Preheat oven to 350°. In large bowl, combine cake mix, pineapple and juice, milk, eggs and oil. Beat on low speed to blend, about 1 minute.

Add bananas and beat on medium speed for 2 minutes.

Pour batter into greased and floured 9" x 13" baking pan. Bake for 30 to 35 minutes, or until cake is lightly browned and tests done. During last 5 minutes of baking, prepare frosting. (You'll frost the cake while it's hot from the oven.)

(continued)

Broiled Coconut Frosting
¾ cup packed brown sugar
⅓ cup (5 ⅓ tablespoons) butter or margarine
2 tablespoons milk
1 cup shredded coconut
½ cup chopped pecans

Set oven to broil. In medium saucepan, cook brown sugar, butter and milk over low to medium heat for 2 minutes, or until butter is melted. Remove from heat and stir in coconut and pecans.

Set oven temperature to broil. Spread mixture over hot cake, and return cake to oven for 2 to 3 minutes, or until lightly browned on top (watch carefully, frosting can easily burn; check after 1 ½ minutes).

CHOCOLATE OATMEAL CAKE

1 ½ cups boiling water
1 cup quick cooking oats
1 cup semi-sweet chocolate chips
1 (18.25 ounce) white cake mix
¼ cup (½ stick) butter or margarine, softened
¼ cup packed brown sugar
3 eggs

Preheat oven to 325°. In small bowl, combine water and oats. Sprinkle chocolate chips over (do not stir), and let stand for 20 minutes.

In large bowl, combine cake mix, butter, brown sugar and eggs and beat on low speed to blend. Add oat mixture and beat on medium speed for 1 minute.

Pour batter into greased and floured 9" x 13" baking pan, and bake for 35 to 40 minutes, or until cake tester comes out clean. Cool and frost with Coffee Frosting.

(continued)

Coffee Frosting
2 teaspoons instant coffee granules
3 tablespoons half-and-half, warmed
½ cup (1 stick) butter or margarine, softened
1 teaspoon vanilla extract
Pinch salt
4 cups powdered sugar

In small bowl, dissolve coffee granules in half-and-half. Set aside.

In medium bowl, cream butter with vanilla and salt. Gradually beat in powdered sugar. Add the coffee mixture and beat well. (If necessary, add small amounts of powdered sugar until frosting reaches spreading consistency.)

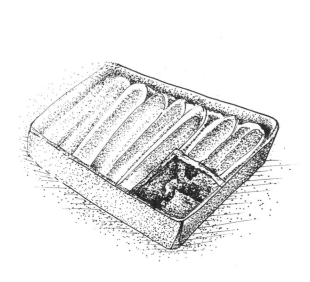

LEMON CREAM CHEESE SWIRL CAKE

⅓ cup sugar
1 (8 ounce) package cream cheese, softened
4 eggs, divided
1 teaspoon lemon extract
1 (18.25 ounce) lemon cake mix, with pudding in the
   mix
1 ¼ cups buttermilk
⅓ cup vegetable oil

Preheat oven to 350°. In medium bowl cream sugar
and cheese until well blended. Beat in 1 egg and
lemon extract until mixture is light and fluffy. Set
aside.

In large bowl, combine cake mix with buttermilk, oil
and 3 eggs. Beat on low speed for 2 to 3 minutes.

Pour batter into greased and floured 9" x 13" baking
pan. Pour cream cheese mixture on top of batter, in
2 rows the length of the pan. Swirl batter gently with
a knife or spatula, taking care not to over mix. Bake
for 30 to 35 minutes, until cake tester comes out
clean. Cool and frost with Lemon Icing.

(continued)

Lemon Icing
1 teaspoon lemon zest (grated lemon rind)
6 tablespoons butter or margarine, softened
3 cups powdered sugar
¼ cup fresh lemon juice

In medium bowl, cream lemon zest and butter until well blended. Add 1 cup powdered sugar, blending until completely incorporated.

Add lemon juice and remaining sugar alternately, blending well after each addition until icing is smooth and reaches frosting consistency.

STRAWBERRY LEMON CAKE WITH FLUFFY CREAM CHEESE FROSTING

This cake combines the tartness of lemons with the sweetness of strawberries. When you make it, you'll want to put the sliced strawberries on top just before serving to keep the juice from the strawberries from seeping out into the icing and discoloring it.

1 (18.25 ounce) white cake mix
1 (3 ounce) package lemon-flavored gelatin
1 ⅓ cups (approx. 16 ounce package) frozen
    strawberries in syrup, thawed
¼ cup vegetable oil
3 eggs

Preheat oven to 350°. In large bowl, combine cake mix, gelatin, strawberries (and syrup), oil and eggs. Beat on low speed until blended, then beat on medium for 2 minutes. Pour batter into greased and floured 9" x 13" baking pan, and bake for 35 minutes, or until cake tester comes out clean. Cool and frost with Fluffy Cream Cheese Frosting.

Fluffy Cream Cheese Frosting
4 ounces cream cheese, softened
¾ cup sugar
4 ounces frozen whipped topping, thawed
1 (8 ounce) container fresh strawberries, sliced

In large bowl, beat cream cheese and sugar until light and fluffy. Fold in whipped topping until thoroughly blended. Frost cake and arrange sliced strawberries attractively on surface for decoration.

BANANA NUT CAKE

1 (18.25 ounce) yellow cake mix
3 eggs
⅓ cup vegetable oil
1 cup milk
3 tablespoons sugar
1 cup mashed ripe bananas (about 2 ½ medium
   bananas)
1 cup chopped black walnuts

Preheat oven to 350°. In large bowl, combine cake mix, eggs, oil, milk and sugar. Beat on low speed to blend, then beat on medium for 2 minutes. Add bananas and beat for 1 more minute on medium. Stir in walnuts. Pour batter into greased and floured 9" x 13" baking pan. Bake for 30 to 35 minutes, or until cake tester comes out clean. Let cake cool until just warm to the touch, and spoon Dark Caramel Glaze over.

Dark Caramel Glaze
1 cup packed dark brown sugar
⅓ cup half-and-half
¼ cup (½ stick) butter or margarine
1 teaspoon vanilla

In medium saucepan, melt brown sugar, half-and-half, and butter over medium heat and bring to a boil. Boil for 6 minutes, stirring constantly until mixture is thickened. Remove from heat; beat in vanilla. Spoon over warm cake as evenly as possible. To ensure adequate coverage, poke holes in top of cake with a toothpick or bamboo skewer before spooning glaze over.

The glaze will have the consistency of a thick syrup.

7-UP CAKE

1 (18.25) lemon cake mix
1 (3.4 ounce) package vanilla flavor instant pudding
1 (8 ounce) can crushed pineapple, drained
1 cup 7-Up
⅔ cup vegetable oil
4 eggs

Preheat oven to 350°. In large bowl, combine cake mix, pudding mix, pineapple, 7-Up, oil and eggs. Beat on low speed to blend, then beat on medium for 3 minutes.

Pour into greased and floured 9" x 13" baking pan. Bake for 30 to 35 minutes, or until cake tester comes out clean. Cool and frost with Coconut Pineapple Frosting.

Coconut Pineapple Frosting
½ cup (1 stick) butter or margarine
1 ½ cups sugar
1 (8 ounce) can crushed pineapple (with juice)
2 tablespoons flour
2 eggs, slightly beaten
1 cup shredded coconut

In medium saucepan, cook butter, sugar, pineapple and juice, flour and eggs over low to medium heat until thickened.

Remove from heat; stir in coconut, and mix well. Spread over cake while still warm.

CINNAMON BUN CAKE

1 (18.25 ounce) butter recipe golden cake mix
¾ cup (1 ½ sticks) butter or margarine, melted
4 eggs
1 (8 ounce) container sour cream
1 cup packed light brown sugar
1 tablespoon cinnamon

Preheat oven to 325°. In medium bowl, beat cake mix, butter, eggs and sour cream on low speed for approximately 1 minute to blend. Pour half the batter into an ungreased 9" x 13" baking pan.

In small bowl, combine the brown sugar and cinnamon, and sprinkle over the batter.

Pour the remaining batter over sugar mixture, and with a knife or spatula swirl sugar mixture in cinnamon bun design.

Bake for 40 minutes. Soon after removing from oven, while cake is still hot, ice with powdered sugar glaze.

Powdered Sugar Glaze
2 cups powdered sugar
4 tablespoons milk
½ teaspoon vanilla extract
½ teaspoon butter extract

In small bowl, mix powdered sugar, milk, vanilla and butter extract until well blended.

HONEY CITRUS CAKE
WITH LEMON GLAZE

With a delicate flavor and the sweetness of honey, this cake makes the perfect light dessert for a Summer get together or brunch.

1 (18.25 ounce) butter recipe golden cake mix (or
　yellow cake mix)
½ cup (1 stick) butter or margarine, softened
3 eggs
⅔ cup orange juice
1 teaspoon lemon zest (grated lemon rind)
Scant ¼ cup powdered sugar, for garnish

Preheat oven to 350°. In large bowl, combine cake mix, butter, eggs, orange juice and lemon zest. Beat on low speed to blend, then beat on medium for 2 minutes.

Pour batter into greased and floured 9" x 13" baking pan, and bake for 30 to 35 minutes, or until cake tester comes out clean. Remove cake from oven and let cool in pan.

When lukewarm, poke holes over surface with toothpick or bamboo skewer, and spoon Lemon Glaze over. When glaze has soaked into cake, sift powdered sugar lightly over for decoration.

Lemon Glaze
⅓ cup fresh lemon juice
½ cup honey

Combine lemon juice and honey in small saucepan. Warm over low heat while stirring until blended.

DIRT AND WORMS CAKE

This fun dessert is easy to make and the younger crowd will love it! This is one mud cake you won't mind them eating! (Also consider this cake for the gardener in your family, and serve it with a plastic toy trowel—no one's ever too old to have fun with her food.)

1 (18.25 ounce) chocolate cake mix (with or without pudding in the mix)
½ cup chocolate syrup
1 (3.9 ounce) package chocolate fudge flavor instant pudding mix
1 ¾ cups milk
1 cup crushed chocolate graham crackers (about 10), or other chocolate cookie
7 candy worms (such as Gummi worms)

Preheat oven to 350°. Prepare cake mix as directed on package for a 9" x 13" cake pan and bake. While cake is still hot from oven, poke holes over entire surface using a bamboo skewer or long tined fork. Pour chocolate syrup evenly over cake, and let cool.

In small bowl, beat pudding mix and milk for two minutes, then let it sit for 3 to 5 minutes more until set. Smooth evenly over cake.

Sprinkle crushed graham crackers over pudding, and scatter worms on top, pushing one end gently into cookie mixture and covering lightly with cookie crumbs, so it appears to be poking out of the ground. Refrigerate until ready to serve.

PEAR CARAMEL RIBBON CAKE

O.K. I have to be honest here. This is one cake I wasn't sure was going to make it into this book. I knew the flavor of caramel, spice and pears would be a good combination, but it didn't turn out exactly as I had planned.

Because I liked the taste, I decided to get some other opinions before jumping to conclusions. So, I sent it to work with my husband the next day to let his co-workers sample it and give me feedback. The verdict came in: it was a keeper. Everyone loved the moist texture of the pear-studded cake, and the flavor added by the caramel ribbon running through its middle.

1 cup (2 sticks) butter or margarine, divided
1 (18.25 ounce) spice cake mix
1 (15.25 ounce) can pears in heavy syrup, drained,
   syrup reserved
1 cup reserved pear syrup
3 eggs
1 (14 ounce) package individually-wrapped caramels
   (about 40 pieces)
½ cup evaporated milk
1 ½ cups chopped pecans, divided
¾ cup packed brown sugar

(continued)

Preheat oven to 350°. Melt ½ cup (1 stick) butter and pour into large bowl. Add cake mix, pear syrup and eggs. Beat on low speed to blend, then beat on medium for 2 minutes. Pour half of batter in greased and floured 9" x 13" baking pan. Bake for 15 minutes, until top of cake is "set."

While cake is baking, prepare caramel. Combine remaining butter, caramels and milk in medium saucepan over low heat. Stir constantly until caramels are melted and mixture is smooth. Pour over baked cake. Sprinkle ¾ cup pecans over. Top with remaining cake batter.

Combine brown sugar and remaining pecans. Sprinkle evenly over batter and return cake to oven for another 35 to 40 minutes, or until cake tester inserted in top half of cake comes out clean. Remove from oven and cool.

APPLE CRANBERRY STREUSEL

This moist cake makes a welcome addition to a breakfast gathering or holiday meal. The apple and cranberry flavors are the perfect complement to each other.

1 (18.25 ounce) yellow cake mix
⅔ cup apple cider (or water)
½ cup (1 stick) butter or margarine, softened
3 eggs
3 cups diced Granny Smith apples (or other baking apple)
¾ cup dried, sweetened cranberries
2 tablespoons flour
Streusel Topping

Preheat oven to 350°. In large bowl, blend cake mix, cider, butter and eggs on low speed for 30 seconds to blend. Then beat at medium speed for three minutes.

In medium bowl, combine apples and cranberries with flour; toss to coat. Gently stir into batter until well mixed. Pour batter into greased and floured 9" x 13" baking dish.

Bake for 30 minutes, remove from oven and sprinkle streusel topping evenly over. Return to oven and bake for another 15 minutes, or until cake tester comes out clean.

(continued)

Streusel Topping
1 cup packed light brown sugar
1 ½ cups flour
¾ cup (1 ½ sticks) butter or margarine, softened
½ cup chopped pecans

 In medium bowl, combine all ingredients, and mix with fork until well blended and crumbly.

KEY LIME PIE CAKE

1 (18.25 ounce) white cake mix
3 eggs
2 tablespoons vegetable oil
1 teaspoon lemon extract
1 ⅓ cups milk
2 cups boiling water
1 (6 ounce) package lime flavor gelatin

Preheat oven to 350°. In large bowl, combine cake mix, eggs, oil, lemon extract and milk. Beat on low speed to blend, then beat on medium for 2 minutes.

Pour batter into greased and floured 9" x 13" baking pan. Bake for 30 to 35 minutes, or until cake tests done. Cool cake in pan, and poke holes over entire surface using a bamboo skewer or long-tined fork.

In medium bowl, stir boiling water into gelatin and stir until gelatin dissolves. Pour over cake, ensuring that cake is evenly covered. Refrigerate cake until well chilled, and frost with Marshmallow Icing.

(continued)

Marshmallow Icing

2 egg whites
⅓ cup water
1 ½ cups sugar
¼ teaspoon cream of tartar
1 tablespoon light corn syrup
2 cups miniature marshmallows (or 16 large
     marshmallows, quartered)
1 teaspoon vanilla, clear

In top of double boiler, combine egg whites, water, sugar, cream of tartar and corn syrup. Beat with hand mixer until stiff peaks form, about 4 minutes. (Be sure to occasionally scrape bottom and sides of pan.) Remove from heat.

Add marshmallows and vanilla, and continue to beat until marshmallows are melted and icing reaches spreading consistency (about 2 minutes).

CHERRY STRUDEL

1 (18.25 ounce) white cake mix, divided
1 cup flour
½ cup sugar
1 (.25 ounce) package dry yeast
⅔ cup warm water
1 teaspoon butter flavoring
2 eggs
1 (21 ounce) can cherry pie filling
⅓ cup butter or margarine, softened

Preheat oven to 375°. In large bowl, combine 1 ½ cups cake mix, flour and sugar. Dissolve yeast in water. Add to dry ingredients in bowl. Stir in butter flavoring and eggs.

Blend thoroughly. Spread batter into greased and floured 9" x 13" baking pan. Spread cherry pie filling over batter.

In small bowl, combine remaining dry cake mix with butter, using fork to blend until crumbly. Sprinkle mixture evenly over pie filling.

Bake for 30 to 35 minutes. Remove from oven, let cool, and drizzle with glaze.

Glaze
1 ½ cups powdered sugar
½ teaspoon almond extract
3 tablespoons warm water

In small bowl, blend sugar, almond extract, and water until smooth.

APPLE CRUMB CAKE

1 (18.25 ounce) yellow cake mix
1 (20 ounce) can apple pie filling
½ cup flour
½ cup packed brown sugar
½ teaspoon cinnamon
¼ cup butter or margarine, softened
½ cup slivered almonds

Preheat oven to 350°. Prepare cake mix as directed on package, except substitute milk for the water (for better consistency). Pour batter into greased and floured 9" x 13" baking pan. Drop pie filling by spoonfuls evenly over cake batter. (Don't stir.)

In medium bowl, combine flour, brown sugar and cinnamon. Stir until blended. Cut in butter with fork or pastry cutter until mixture is crumbly. Stir in almonds. Sprinkle mixture over batter and apples.

Bake for 1 hour, or until cake tester comes out clean. Cool and drizzle with Powdered Sugar Icing.

Powdered Sugar Icing
4 teaspoons warm water
1 cup powdered sugar

In small bowl, stir water into powdered sugar until mixture is smooth.

CHERRY ALMOND STRUDEL

1 (18.25 ounce) lemon cake mix, with pudding in the
   mix
¼ cup (½ stick) butter or margarine, softened
1 (3 ounce) package cream cheese, softened
⅓ cup water
½ teaspoon almond extract
2 eggs
1 (21 ounce) can cherry pie filling
½ cup chopped almonds

Preheat oven to 350°. In large bowl, combine cake
mix, butter and cream cheese. Beat at low speed
until crumbly. Reserve 1 cup of crumb mixture for
topping and set aside.

Add water, almond extract and eggs to remaining
crumb mixture, and beat on high speed for 2
minutes. (The batter will become very smooth and
fluffy.) Spread in greased and floured 9" x 13"
baking pan.

Gently spread cherry pie filling over batter,
smoothing carefully to evenly distribute.

Mix almonds with reserved crumb mixture, and
sprinkle over pie filling.

Bake for 35 minutes, or until cake tester inserted in
center comes out clean and edges are nicely
browned. Remove from oven and let cool for about
half an hour. Drizzle glaze over warm cake.

(continued)

Glaze

½ cup powdered sugar
1 tablespoon butter or margarine, softened
2 to 3 teaspoons milk or cream
¼ teaspoon almond extract

In small bowl, combine sugar, margarine, milk and almond extract. Blend well.

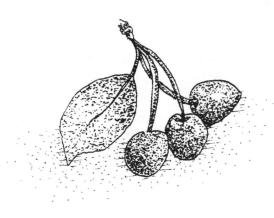

RICOTTA RAISIN CAKE

Because the cheese and raisins form a layer beneath the cake as it bakes, I like to serve the slices upside-down, so that the raisins dot the top of the cake and the cheese layer forms a kind of topping. For especially good flavor, serve the cake warm.

1 (18.25 ounce) lemon cake mix
1 (15 ounce) container ricotta cheese
4 eggs
1 cup sugar
1 teaspoon cinnamon
1 teaspoon vanilla
1 cup raisins
1 tablespoon orange zest (grated orange rind)

Preheat oven to 325°. Prepare cake mix according to package directions, substituting milk for water. Pour batter into greased and floured 9" x 13" baking pan.

In large bowl, combine cheese, eggs, sugar, cinnamon and vanilla. Beat on low speed for 1 to 2 minutes to blend. Stir in raisins and orange zest.

Spoon mixture evenly over cake batter. Bake for 1 hour, or until cake tester comes out clean. Cool slightly and serve with Rum Sauce spooned over.

(continued)

Rum Sauce
⅓ cup butter or margarine
⅔ cup sugar
⅓ cup half-and-half
2 tablespoons rum
1 teaspoon vanilla

Combine butter, sugar and half-and-half in medium saucepan. Cook over medium heat, stirring constantly, until butter is melted and mixture is slightly thickened (about 5 minutes).

Stir in rum and vanilla, and cook for a few minutes more. Let cool slightly and serve over cake.

LEMON CAKE

This cake is very moist, with a tangy lemon flavor. The topping finishes it off with very little effort and really enhances the flavor of the cake. It's sweet, but not overly rich.

1 (18.25 ounce) lemon cake mix
1 (20 ounce) can crushed pineapple, with juice
3 eggs
⅓ cup vegetable oil

Preheat oven to 350°. In large bowl, combine cake mix, pineapple with juice, eggs and oil. Blend on low speed to moisten, then beat on medium for 2 minutes.

Pour batter into greased and floured 9" x 13" baking pan. Bake for 30 minutes. Remove from oven, and spread topping evenly over.

Return cake to oven and bake for an additional 10 minutes. Cool. Keep refrigerated.

Topping
1 (14 ounce) can sweetened condensed milk
1 cup sour cream
¼ cup fresh lemon juice

In medium bowl, combine sweetened condensed milk, sour cream and lemon juice. Stir well to blend.

EARTHQUAKE CAKE

An outrageously delicious cake — you'll be hooked
after your first bite. It makes a great
"1-step" cake because it needs no frosting
(and if you have any doubts, try it).

1 cup coconut
1 cup chopped pecans
½ cup white chocolate chips
1 (18.25 ounce) devil's food cake mix
1 (8 ounce) package cream cheese, softened
½ cup (1 stick) butter or margarine
1 (1 lb.) box powdered sugar
1 teaspoon vanilla

Prheat oven to 350°. Sprinkle coconut, pecans and white chocolate chips evenly in the bottom of a lightly greased 9" x 13" baking pan. Mix cake according to package directions, and pour over mixture in pan.

In medium bowl, thoroughly blend cream cheese, butter, powdered sugar and vanilla. Drop by spoonfuls onto cake mixture, covering entire surface, but do not stir. Bake for 40 to 45 minutes.

APRICOT RASPBERRY
UPSIDE DOWN CAKE

6 tablespoons butter or margarine, melted
1 cup packed light brown sugar
1 (21 ounce) can apricots in heavy syrup, drained and
   sliced, reserve ¾ cup syrup
1 cup frozen raspberries
1 (18.25 ounce) white cake mix
3 tablespoons vegetable oil
⅓ cup milk
3 eggs

Preheat oven to 350°. Pour melted butter in 9" x 13"
baking pan. Sprinkle brown sugar evenly over. Place
apricot slices evenly over brown sugar, and arrange
raspberries around apricots. Set aside.

In large bowl, combine cake mix, reserved apricot
syrup, oil, milk and eggs. Beat on low speed to
blend, then beat on medium for about 2 minutes.

Pour batter carefully over apricots and raspberries,
ensuring they are evenly covered. Bake for 30 to 35
minutes, until cake tester comes out clean.
Immediately upon removing from oven, turn cake
out of pan onto cookie sheet or cake board. Let pan
rest upside-down for 1 minute before removing it to
allow all of topping to drip onto cake. Let cake cool
and serve warm or cold. Refrigerate to keep fresh.

PINEAPPLE UPSIDE DOWN CAKE

This classic couldn't be easier—it ices itself!
Also, for a more robust citrus flavor, substitute
lemon cake mix for the white.

6 tablespoons butter or margarine
1 (20 ounce) can pineapple, either sliced or crushed,
    juice reserved
¾ cup reserved pineapple juice
½ cup chopped pecans
1 ⅓ cups packed light brown sugar
1 (18.25 ounce) white cake mix

Preheat oven to 350°. Melt butter in 9" x 13" baking pan. Drain pineapple, reserving ¾ cup juice. Sprinkle nuts in bottom of pan, and cover evenly with brown sugar. Arrange pineapple slices (or crushed pineapple) on top.

Prepare the cake mix according to package directions, replacing ¾ cup liquid with reserved pineapple juice. Pour over brown sugar, and bake for 45-50 minutes, or until cake top springs back when touched.

SELF-FROSTING
MEXICAN CHOCOLATE CAKE

What a fun and easy cake. The marshmallow mixture cooks to a pudding-like consistency with an intense chocolate flavor. (This cake will appeal to those who prefer less rich frostings.)

2 ½ cups mini marshmallows
1 cup packed brown sugar
½ cup cocoa powder
2 cups hot water
1 (18.25 ounce) devil's food cake mix
1 ⅓ cups buttermilk
3 eggs
⅓ cup vegetable oil
2 teaspoons cinnamon
1 teaspoon vanilla
1 (1 ounce) square unsweetened chocolate, melted
½ cup pecans, chopped and toasted

Preheat oven to 350°. Sprinkle marshmallows evenly in bottom of greased and floured 9" x 13" baking pan. In medium bowl, mix sugar, cocoa and hot water. Pour over marshmallows.

In large bowl, combine cake mix, buttermilk, eggs, oil, cinnamon, vanilla and melted chocolate. Beat on low speed to blend, then beat on medium for 3 minutes. Pour batter evenly over marshmallow mixture.

(continued)

 Bake for 45 minutes, or until cake tester inserted into top half of cake comes out clean. Remove pan from oven and let cool for 20 to 30 minutes. Turn cake out of pan onto serving tray. Use butter knife or spatula to smooth frosting on sides and top of cake. Sprinkle pecans evenly over top.

CHERRY COLA CAKE

What could be better than a chocolate cake loaded with cherry flavor and topped with sweet cherries? This easy cake is another good standby when you need a quick, delicious cake with little fuss or effort. When you turn it out of the pan, it's ready to go, with the cherries on top forming an attractive and tasteful "icing." Since you don't have to worry about frosting getting messed up while you're carrying it, this is a great cake to take to get togethers.

2 (15 ounce) cans dark sweet cherries, pitted, drained, syrup reserved
¾ cup reserved cherry syrup
2 (3 ounce) packages cherry flavor gelatin, divided
1 cup cola, divided
⅛ teaspoon almond extract
2 cups miniature marshmallows
1 (18.25 ounce) German chocolate cake mix
½ cup vegetable oil
4 eggs

Preheat oven to 350°. Arrange cherries in bottom of greased and floured 9" x 13" baking pan.

In small saucepan, combine cherry syrup, 1 package gelatin and ¼ cup cola. Stir over low heat until gelatin is dissolved. Add almond extract and remove from heat to cool slightly.

Pour over cherries, then sprinkle evenly with marshmallows.

(continued)

In large bowl, combine cake mix, 1 package gelatin, oil, eggs and ¾ cup cola. Beat on high speed for 3 minutes.

Carefully spread batter over marshmallows. Bake for 40 to 45 minutes, until cake tester comes out clean.

Remove from oven and cool for about 45 minutes. Turn out of pan onto serving plate. Chill before serving, and keep refrigerated.

RASPBERRY RUM-RAISIN CAKE

¾ cup raisins
¾ cup light rum
3 eggs
½ cup water
¼ cup vegetable oil
1 (3 ounce) package raspberry flavor gelatin
1 (18.25 ounce) box white cake mix

Cover raisins with rum and soak for several hours to plump them up, then drain, reserving rum.

Preheat oven to 350°.

In medium bowl, beat eggs until foamy, about two minutes. Add water, oil, and reserved rum and beat on medium speed. While continuing to beat, slowly add raspberry gelatin and then cake mix, a little at a time, until fully incorporated. Beat for 2 minutes.

Gently stir raisins into batter, then pour batter into greased and floured 12-cup capacity Bundt cake pan. Bake for 45 minutes, or until cake tester comes out clean. Cool for 15 minutes, and then turn cake out of pan.

Cool and frost with Rum Glaze.

You don't have to soak the raisins if you're short on time, just add them right out of the package.

(continued)

Rum Glaze
1 cup (2 sticks) butter
¼ cup water
1 cup sugar
½ cup rum

 In medium saucepan, bring butter, water and sugar
to a boil. Boil for 5 minutes, stirring constantly.
Remove from heat; stir in rum. Spoon over cake.

PINEAPPLE RUM CAKE

1 (18.25 ounce) yellow cake mix
1 (3.4 ounce) package vanilla flavor instant pudding
1 (8 ounce) can crushed pineapple with juice
4 eggs
½ cup rum
⅓ cup vegetable oil

Preheat oven to 350°. In large bowl, combine cake mix, pudding mix, pineapple and juice, eggs, rum and oil. Beat on low speed to blend, then beat on medium for 2 minutes.

Pour batter into greased and floured 12-cup capacity Bundt cake pan, and bake for 50 to 55 minutes, or until cake tester comes out clean.

Cool in pan for 10 minutes, then turn out onto serving platter. Poke holes about ½" apart over surface of cake using either bamboo skewer or long-tined fork. Spoon Butter Rum Glaze over.

(continued)

Butter Rum Glaze
½ cup butter
¼ cup water
1 cup sugar
½ cup rum

In medium saucepan, melt butter over low heat. Add water and sugar, stirring to blend thoroughly. Bring to a boil, and boil for 5 minutes.

Remove from heat, and stir in rum. Let cool slightly and spoon over cake, picking up glaze that pools around bottom of cake and spooning over again so cake absorbs as much as possible.

You can use margarine instead of butter for the glaze, but it really won't taste as good. Since this is the finishing touch on the cake, you want to make it taste as good as it can.

PUMPKIN RUM CAKE

This dense cake is very moist and keeps really well. There's just enough rum in the mix to give a hint of rum flavor to the cake, which goes well with the pumpkin. And its vibrant orange color will add a festive look to any table, especially at Thanksgiving.

1 (18.25 ounce) white cake mix
1 (15 ounce) can pumpkin
3 eggs
½ cup rum
¾ cup chopped pecans, toasted

Preheat oven to 325⁰. In large bowl, combine cake mix, pumpkin, eggs and rum. Beat on low speed to blend, then beat on medium for 2 minutes. Stir in pecans until well-blended.

Pour batter into greased and floured 12-cup capacity Bundt cake pan. Bake for 45 to 50 minutes, or until cake tester comes out clean.

Let cake cool in pan for 10 minutes, then turn out onto serving platter and frost with Orange Glaze.

Orange Glaze
1 cup powdered sugar
2 tablespoons, plus ½ teaspoon orange juice
1 tablespoon orange zest (grated orange rind)

Mix powdered sugar, orange juice and orange zest until smooth. Spoon over top of cake, letting icing run down the sides.

ORANGE BUNDT CAKE WITH CITRUS RUM SAUCE

1 (18.25 ounce) butter recipe golden cake mix
3 eggs
⅔ cup orange juice
½ cup (1 stick) butter or margarine, softened
4 tablespoons orange zest

Preheat oven to 350⁰. In large bowl, combine cake mix, eggs, orange juice, butter and orange zest. Beat on low speed to blend, then beat on medium for 3 minutes.

Pour batter into greased and floured 12-cup capacity Bundt cake pan, and bake for 45 to 50 minutes, or until cake tester comes out clean.

Cool cake slightly in pan, then leaving cake in pan, poke holes ½" apart over entire surface of cake using bamboo skewer or long-tined fork. Spoon Citrus Rum Sauce evenly over, letting it soak into cake. Leave cake in pan for another 2 hours to absorb sauce, then turn out onto serving plate and dust with powdered sugar.

Citrus Rum Sauce
½ cup sugar
¼ cup water
¼ cup orange juice
2 tablespoons lemon juice
2 tablespoons rum

Combine sugar and water in medium saucepan and bring to a boil. Boil for 1 minute, stirring frequently, and remove from heat. Cool slightly. Stir in orange juice, lemon juice and rum.

COCONUT FILLED CHOCOLATE CAKE

The white coconut running through the center looks pretty against the dark chocolate cake.

1 (18.25 ounce) devil's food cake mix, batter prepared
   as directed on package (substitute buttermilk for
   water called for in directions for richer consistency)
1 egg white
¼ cup sugar
1 cup shredded coconut
1 tablespoon flour
1 teaspoon vanilla (clear)

Preheat oven to 350⁰. In medium bowl, beat egg white until soft peaks form. Gradually add sugar and continue to beat until stiff peaks form. Fold in coconut, flour, and vanilla.

Pour half of prepared cake mix batter into greased and floured 12-cup capacity Bundt cake pan.

Drop coconut filling by spoonful evenly over center of batter in pan, avoiding touching the sides.

Pour remaining batter over and smooth top.

Bake for 45 minutes, or until cake tester comes out clean. Cool cake in pan for 10 minutes, then turn out onto cooling rack. When cool, ice with Milk Chocolate Glaze.

(continued)

Milk Chocolate Glaze
⅓ cup evaporated milk
¾ cup milk chocolate chips

 In medium saucepan, melt chocolate chips in milk over medium heat. (Mixture will be thin.) Cool to lukewarm and spoon over cake, covering entire surface.

If you're using shortening and flour to grease the pan, use cocoa powder in place of the flour to give a nice even color on the cake's surface when it comes out of the pan.

SPICY WALNUT RUM CAKE

1 (18.25 ounce) spice cake mix
4 eggs
1 ⅓ cups buttermilk
⅓ cup vegetable oil
½ cup packed brown sugar
1 ½ cups chopped walnuts, toasted

Preheat oven to 325°. In large bowl, combine cake mix, eggs, buttermilk, oil and brown sugar. Beat on low speed to blend, then beat on medium for 2 minutes. Stir in walnuts until well blended.

Pour batter into greased and floured 12-cup capacity Bundt cake pan. Bake for 50 to 55 minutes, or until cake tester comes out clean.

Remove from oven, and cool in pan for 10 minutes. Leave in pan and poke holes over entire surface of cake bottom using a bamboo skewer or a long tined fork. Using a large spoon, spoon Rum Syrup evenly over, letting it soak in after each spoonful. Let cake remain in pan until fully cool, about 2 hours, then turn out onto serving platter.

(continued)

Rum Syrup
1 cup rum
1 cup sugar
¼ cup (½ stick) butter or margarine

 Combine rum, sugar and butter in medium saucepan. Bring to a simmer, stirring frequently, and cook for 2 minutes. Remove from heat and spoon over cake.

You can use margarine for the Rum Syrup, but it doesn't taste as good as butter. I always use butter when I make this.

ANISETTE EASTER CAKE

*This cake is a version of an Italian Easter cake that my mother
makes from a recipe handed down from her father, who came from
Rome. The original cake has a more bread-like texture; it's very
dense and less sweet. It's a family tradition to eat the cakes on
Easter morning with butter and capicola, a cured Italian ham.*

*This dessert version is much quicker to make
(you don't have to let the cakes rise!).*

1 (18.25 ounce) white cake mix
1 (3.4 ounce) vanilla flavor instant pudding mix
¼ cup sugar
3 eggs
⅓ cup half-and-half (or light cream)
⅓ cup vegetable oil
⅔ cup anisette
3 tablespoons anise seeds*
2 tablespoons lemon juice
1 tablespoon lemon zest (grated lemon rind)

Preheat oven to 350⁰. In large bowl, combine cake
mix, pudding mix, sugar, eggs, half-and-half, oil,
anisette mixture, lemon juice and zest. Beat on low
speed to blend, then beat on medium for 2 minutes.
Pour batter into greased and floured 12-cup capacity
Bundt pan.

Bake for 50 minutes, or until cake tester comes out
clean. Let cool for 10 minutes in pan, then turn out
onto cooling rack. When cool, ice with Butter Lemon
Icing.

(continued)

Butter Lemon Icing
3 tablespoons butter, softened
1 cup powdered sugar
1 tablespoon lemon zest (grated lemon rind)
3 teaspoons half-and-half (or light cream)

In medium bowl, cream butter with sugar until smooth. Add lemon zest, and blend. Add-half-and half one teaspoon at a time, blending well after each addition. (This recipe makes enough icing to frost the crown of the cake. You can double the recipe if you want to frost the entire cake.)

* Soak the anise seeds in the anisette overnight or longer, to soften them. I usually put them in a small container with a tight-fitting lid. Add the anise seeds to the anisette, stir to mix, then cover. You can soak the seeds for several days, if you want.

APRICOT BRANDY CAKE

1 (18.25 ounce) yellow cake mix
1 (3.4 oz) lemon flavor pudding mix
4 eggs
1 cup sour cream
½ cup brandy
1 (15.25 ounce) can apricot halves, sliced

 Preheat oven to 350°. In large bowl, combine cake mix, pudding mix, eggs, sour cream and brandy. Beat on low speed to blend, then beat on medium for 2 minutes more. Gently fold in apricot slices.

Pour batter into greased and floured 12-cup capacity Bundt cake pan. Bake for 50 to 55 minutes, or until cake tester comes out clean.

Cool in pan for 10 minutes, then turn out onto serving platter. When cool, sprinkle with powdered sugar.

AMARETTO CAKE

1 (18.25 ounce) white cake mix
1 (3.4 ounce) vanilla flavor instant pudding mix
4 eggs
6 teaspoons amaretto liqueur
½ cup water
½ cup vegetable oil
½ cup sliced almonds

Preheat oven to 350°. In large bowl, combine cake mix, pudding mix, eggs, amaretto, water and oil. Beat on low speed to blend, then beat on medium speed for 2 minutes.

Sprinkle almonds into bottom of greased and floured 12-cup capacity Bundt cake pan. Pour batter over almonds.

Bake for 40 to 45 minutes, or until cake tester comes out clean. Remove from oven, poke holes over bottom of cake (using bamboo skewer or long-tined fork), and pour amaretto icing evenly over, letting it soak into holes. Leave cake in pan for at least 2 hours before removing, to give icing a chance to soak into cake.

Amaretto Icing
½ cup amaretto liqueur
1 cup powdered sugar

In medium bowl, combine amaretto with sugar, blending until mixture is smooth.

LEMON BLUEBERRY BUNDT CAKE WITH HONEY LEMON GLAZE

1 (18.25 ounce) lemon cake mix
1 (3.4 ounce) vanilla flavor instant pudding mix
1 (8 ounce) container vanilla yogurt
3 eggs
⅓ cup oil
2 cups blueberries, fresh or frozen
2 tablespoons flour

Preheat oven to 350⁰. In large bowl, combine cake mix, pudding mix, yogurt, eggs and oil. Beat on low speed to blend, then beat on medium for 2 minutes.

In small bowl, toss blueberries gently with flour to coat. Stir carefully into batter.

Pour batter into greased and floured 12-cup capacity Bundt cake pan. Bake for 50 to 55 minutes, or until cake tester comes out clean. Cool cake in pan for 10 minutes, then turn out onto serving platter. Let cool, and spoon Honey Lemon Glaze over.

(continued)

Honey Lemon Glaze
2 tablespoons sugar
¼ cup honey
1 tablespoon lemon juice
1 tablespoon butter

In small saucepan, bring sugar, honey, lemon juice, and butter to a boil, stirring constantly. Boil gently for 1 minute; remove from heat. Let cool for several minutes, then spoon over cake.

After spooning the glaze over the cake, I generally scoop up some of the glaze that has pooled around the bottom of the cake and spoon it over the cake again, covering places that were missed the first time. Not only does this cover the cake better, but it also gives the glaze a chance to soak into the cake a little bit.

APRICOT STREUSEL BUNDT CAKE

1 (18.25 ounce) yellow cake mix
1 (3.4 ounce) package vanilla flavor instant pudding
   mix
1 (15.25 ounce) can apricot halves in heavy syrup,
   drained, sliced, reserve syrup
1 cup reserved apricot syrup
4 eggs
½ cup vegetable oil
½ cup packed brown sugar
2 teaspoons cinnamon
½ cup finely chopped pecans

Preheat oven to 350°. In large bowl, combine cake mix, pudding mix, apricot syrup, eggs and oil. Beat on low speed to blend, then beat on medium for 2 minutes.

In small bowl, combine sugar, cinnamon and pecans; mix well.

Pour half of batter into greased and floured 12-cup capacity Bundt cake pan. Place half of sliced apricots evenly over batter, and sprinkle half of sugar mixture over.

Gently pour remaining batter on top, and smooth over. Layer other half of apricots and sprinkle with remaining sugar mixture. Bake for 55-60 minutes, or until cake tester comes out clean. Cool in pan for 10 minutes, then turn out onto cooling rack. Ice with Powdered Sugar Glaze.

(continued)

Powdered Sugar Glaze

¾ cup powdered sugar
½ teaspoon vanilla (clear)
3 teaspoons warm water

 In small bowl, mix sugar, vanilla and water. If needed, add water a couple of drops at a time as needed until icing reaches drizzling consistency.

 Drizzle over cake, using a knife to spread more evenly on the top of cake, and let it run down the sides. (Note: You need to work fast with this glaze, because it hardens quickly.)

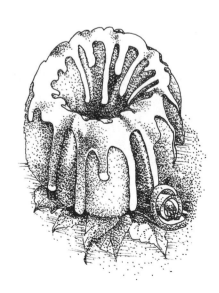

ORANGE-TOPPED
LEMON BUNDT CAKE

1 (18 ounce) jar orange marmalade
⅔ cup shredded coconut
6 tablespoons butter or margarine, melted
1 (18.25 ounce) yellow cake mix
1 (3.4 ounce) lemon flavor instant pudding mix
4 eggs
1 cup orange juice
⅓ cup vegetable oil

Preheat oven to 350°. In small bowl, combine orange marmalade, coconut and butter. Mix well. Pour mixture into bottom of greased and floured 12-cup capacity Bundt cake pan.

In large bowl, combine cake mix, pudding mix, eggs, orange juice and oil. Beat on low speed to blend, then beat on medium speed for 2 minutes.

Pour batter over orange mixture in pan. Bake for 50 to 60 minutes, or until cake tests done. Cool in pan for 10 minutes, then turn out onto serving plate.

You can substitute the orange marmalade with pineapple preserves for a nice change. They have a sharper citrus flavor that goes really well with the flavors of lemon and orange in the cake.

BLUEBERRY CREAM CHEESE CAKE

1 (18.25 ounce) yellow cake mix
4 eggs
½ cup milk
¼ cup vegetable oil
½ cup sugar
1 teaspoon almond extract
1 (8 ounce) package cream cheese, softened
1 ½ cups blueberries, fresh or frozen
1 tablespoon flour
Powdered sugar, for decoration

Preheat oven to 350°. In large bowl, combine cake mix, eggs, milk, oil, sugar and almond extract. Beat on low speed to blend. Add cream cheese and beat on medium for 2 minutes. In small bowl, toss blueberries with flour to coat. Gently stir into batter.

Pour batter into greased and floured 12-cup capacity Bundt cake pan, and bake for 50 to 55 minutes, or until cake tester comes out clean. Cool in pan for 10 minutes, then turn out onto serving platter. Dust with powdered sugar, if desired.

NEVER-ENDING
CHOCOLATE BUNDT CAKE

1 (18.25 ounce) devil's food cake mix
1 (3.9 ounce) package dark fudge instant pudding mix
1 ¼ cups buttermilk
½ cup vegetable oil
½ cup chocolate syrup
4 eggs
1 cup semi-sweet chocolate chips

Preheat oven to 325°. In large bowl, combine cake
mix, pudding mix, milk, oil, syrup and eggs. Beat on
low speed to blend, then beat on medium speed for 2
to 3 minutes. Gently stir in chocolate chips and pour
batter into greased and floured 12-cup capacity
Bundt cake pan.

Bake for 55 minutes to 1 hour, or until cake tester
comes out clean. Let cake cool in pan for 10
minutes, and then turn out onto cooling rack.
Sprinkle with powdered sugar for garnish, or drizzle
with Chocolate Glaze.

*To make it look extra special, drizzle white over the dark
chocolate glaze. It adds a lot of pizzazz for a professional-looking
touch.*

(continued)

Chocolate Glaze
1 cup semi-sweet chocolate chips
⅔ cup evaporated milk

Combine chocolate and milk in small saucepan. Cook and stir over low heat until blended and mixture comes to a boil. Lower heat and cook, stirring constantly until thickened.

White Chocolate Drizzling Glaze
¼ cup white chocolate baking chips, melted

For a quick and easy way to drizzle the glaze: put the melted chocolate in a plastic bag (like a sandwich bag) and snip off a corner. Then squeeze the bag gently to drizzle the chocolate.

WHITE CHOCOLATE BUNDT CAKE

2 cups white chocolate chips, divided
1 cup milk
1 (18.25 ounce) white cake mix
1 (3.3 ounce) white chocolate flavor instant pudding
    mix (or vanilla flavor, if the white chocolate isn't
    available)
4 eggs
⅓ cup vegetable oil
1 tablespoon flour

Preheat oven to 350°. In small saucepan, combine 1
cup baking chips with milk and melt over low heat,
stirring constantly, until mixture is smooth. Remove
from heat and cool.

In large bowl, combine cake mix, pudding mix,
chocolate mixture, eggs and oil. Beat on low speed to
moisten, then on medium speed for 2 minutes, until
thoroughly blended.

Coat remaining baking chips with flour and stir into
batter. Pour batter into greased and floured 12-cup
capacity Bundt cake pan, and bake for 50 minutes,
or until cake tester comes out clean. Frost with
White Chocolate Icing.

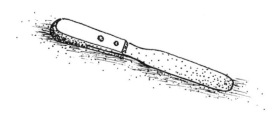

(continued)

White Chocolate Icing

¾ cup white chocolate baking chips
1 tablespoon flour
½ cup milk
½ cup (1 stick) butter or margarine
1 cup powdered sugar
1 teaspoon vanilla

In small saucepan, combine baking chips, flour and milk; cook over medium heat, stirring constantly, until chocolate is completely melted and mixture thickens (about 3 minutes). Remove from heat and cool.

In medium bowl, combine margarine, powdered sugar and vanilla; beat until light and fluffy (about 2 minutes). Slowly add white chocolate mixture, and beat until well blended.

CRANBERRY ORANGE BUNDT CAKE

1 (18.25 ounce) butter recipe golden cake mix
3 eggs
⅔ cup orange juice
½ cup (1 stick) butter or margarine, softened
¼ cup sugar
1 (8 ounce) package cream cheese, softened
Zest of one medium orange (about 2 tablespoons)
1 ½ cups dried sweetened cranberries
1 tablespoon flour

Preheat oven to 350°. In large bowl, combine cake mix, eggs, orange juice, butter and sugar. Beat on low speed to blend. Add cream cheese and orange zest, and beat for 2 minutes.

In medium bowl, toss cranberries with flour to coat; stir into batter.

Pour batter into greased and floured 12-cup capacity Bundt cake pan, and bake for 50 to 55 minutes, or until cake tester comes out clean. Cool in pan for 10 minutes, then turn out onto serving plate. When completely cool, top with Orange Glaze.

(continued)

Orange Glaze

½ cup sugar
½ cup water
1 ½ tablespoons cornstarch
Pinch salt
1 ½ tablespoons orange zest (grated orange rind)
1 tablespoon butter or margarine
¼ cup orange juice

In medium saucepan, combine sugar, water, cornstarch and salt. Cook over medium heat, stirring frequently, until mixture comes to a boil. Boil for 1 minute, stirring constantly.

Remove from heat, and stir in orange zest and butter. Gradually stir in orange juice.

Place back over medium heat, bring to a simmer and cook for 3 to 4 minutes until thickened. Remove from heat and cool. Spoon over cooled cake.

CHERRY CORDIAL CAKE

3 eggs
¼ cup water
½ cup vegetable oil
1 (18.25 ounce) white cake mix
1 (3 ounce) package cherry flavor instant gelatin
¾ cup reserved maraschino cherry juice
1 (16 ounce) jar maraschino cherries, drained and
coarsely-chopped

Preheat oven to 350°. Beat eggs on high speed until foamy, about 2 minutes. Blend water and oil with eggs. Slowly add cake mix and gelatin, beating constantly. Add maraschino cherry juice and beat for two minutes more.

Gently stir maraschino cherries into batter.

Pour batter into greased and floured 12-cup capacity Bundt cake pan, and bake for approximately 45 minutes or until cake tester comes out clean. When cool, ice with chocolate glaze.

Chocolate Glaze
6 (1 ounce) squares semi-sweet baking chocolate
⅔ cup evaporated milk

In small saucepan, combine chocolate and evaporated milk. Cook and stir over low heat until until mixture comes to a boil. Lower heat and cook gently for 3 to 5 minutes, stirring constantly until thickened. Cool, stirring occasionally.

DATE SPICE CAKE
WITH BROWN SUGAR GLAZE

1 (18.25 ounce) spice cake mix
4 eggs
1 cup sour cream
⅓ cup vegetable oil
½ cup molasses
¾ cup chopped dates
¾ cup chopped walnuts

Preheat oven to 325°. In large bowl, combine cake mix, eggs, sour cream, oil and molasses. Beat on low speed to blend, then beat on medium speed for 2 minutes.

Stir in dates and walnuts. Pour batter into greased and floured 12-cup capacity Bundt cake pan. Bake for 50 to 55 minutes, or until cake tester comes out clean. Cool in pan for 10 minutes, then turn out onto cooling rack. Cool and ice with Brown Sugar Glaze.

Brown Sugar Glaze
¼ cup (½ stick) butter or margarine
¼ cup packed brown sugar
2 tablespoons milk
1 teaspoon vanilla
1 cup powdered sugar

In small saucepan, combine butter, brown sugar and milk. Bring to a boil, stirring frequently. Remove from heat and stir in vanilla. Beat in powdered sugar. Let cool for a couple of minutes, and then spoon over cake, letting icing run down the sides.

ORANGE WALNUT COFFEE CAKE

1 (18.25 ounce) yellow cake mix
3 eggs
1 (8 ounce) container sour cream
⅓ cup orange juice
Zest of one large orange
½ cup chopped walnuts

Preheat oven to 350°. Mix cake mix, eggs, sour cream, orange juice and orange zest on low speed to blend, then beat on medium for 2 minutes.

Gently stir walnuts into batter. Pour batter into greased and floured 12-cup capacity Bundt cake pan.

Bake for 40 to 45 minutes, or until cake tester comes out clean. Cool in pan for 10 minutes, then turn out onto cooling rack. When cool, spoon Orange Icing over.

Orange Icing
2 tablespoons butter or margarine, softened
1 cup powdered sugar, divided
2 tablespoons orange juice
1 teaspoon orange zest (grated orange rind)

In small bowl, cream butter with half the powdered sugar. Add orange juice and zest, mix well. Gradually beat in remaining powdered sugar until icing is smooth. (The icing will have a somewhat thin consistency, which allows it to flow down the sides of the cake when you spoon it over the top.)

COCONUT CAKE

1 (18.25 ounce) box white cake mix
1 (3.4 ounce) package coconut cream flavor pudding
   mix
4 eggs
2 tablespoons vegetable oil
1 cup cream of coconut
¾ cup milk
2 cups shredded coconut

Preheat oven to 350°. Combine cake mix, pudding mix, eggs, oil, cream of coconut and milk on low speed for 30 seconds, then beat on medium for 2 minutes.

Fold in coconut and pour into greased and floured 12-cup capacity Bundt pan. Bake for 1 hour, or until cake tests done. Cool cake and ice with Chocolate Glaze.

Chocolate Glaze
6 ounces sweet baking chocolate
Scant ⅓ cup heavy cream
2 tablespoons corn syrup
1 tablespoon sugar

In small saucepan, melt chocolate, cream, corn syrup and sugar over low heat until blended. Remove from heat and cool slightly.

WATERGATE CAKE

1 (18.25 ounce) box white cake mix
1 (3.4 oz) package pistachio flavor instant pudding
  mix
½ cup vegetable oil
½ cup milk
4 eggs
1 (8 ounce) can crushed pineapple with juice
1 cup mini-marshmallows
½ cup chopped pecans
½ cup shredded coconut

Preheat oven to 350°. In large bowl, combine cake
mix, pudding mix, oil, milk, eggs and pineapple with
juice. Beat on low speed for 30 seconds to blend,
then beat on medium for 2 minutes.

Gently stir in marshmallows, pecans and coconut.

Pour batter into a greased and floured 12-cup
capacity Bundt pan, and bake for 45 to 50 minutes,
or until cake tests done.

If desired, serve with a dollop of whipped cream.

APPLE CIDER BUNDT CAKE

1 (18.25 ounce) yellow cake mix
½ cup butter or margarine, melted
3 eggs
1 ⅓ cups apple cider
1 teaspoon cinnamon
½ teaspoon allspice

Preheat oven to 350°. In large bowl, combine cake mix, butter, eggs, cider, cinnamon and allspice. Beat on low speed to blend, then beat on medium for 2 minutes.

Pour batter into greased and floured 12-cup capacity Bundt cake pan, and bake for 45 to 50 minutes, or until cake tester comes out clean.

Cool in pan for 10 minutes, then turn out onto serving platter or cooling rack.

FRUIT COCKTAIL STREUSEL CAKE

Streusel mixture
½ cup flour
1 cup shredded coconut
1 cup quick cooking oats
¾ cup packed brown sugar
½ cup chopped pecans
½ cup (1 stick) butter or margarine, softened

Cake
1 (18.25 ounce) butter recipe golden cake mix
1 (3.4 ounce) package lemon flavor instant pudding
   mix
1 (16 ounce) can fruit cocktail, drained, syrup
   reserved
4 eggs
¼ cup vegetable oil

Preheat oven to 325°. Prepare streusel mixture. In medium bowl combine flour, coconut, oats, brown sugar and pecans. Mix well. Cut in margarine until mixture is crumbly. Set aside.

In large bowl, combine cake mix, pudding mix, reserved syrup, eggs and oil. Beat on medium high speed for 3 minutes. Gently fold in fruit and mix well.

Pour ⅓ batter into greased and floured 12-cup capacity Bundt cake pan. Sprinkle ⅓ streusel mixture over. Repeat twice more, ending with streusel mixture.

Bake for 1 hour, or until cake tester comes out clean. Cool cake in pan for 10 minutes, then turn out onto cooling rack. When cool, spoon Butter Glaze over.

(continued)

Butter Glaze
½ cup (1 stick) butter
½ cup sugar
½ cup evaporated milk
1 cup shredded coconut

In small saucepan, combine butter, sugar and evaporated milk. Bring to a boil.

Add coconut and boil for 5 to 6 minutes, stirring frequently, until thickened. Remove from heat and let cool slightly.

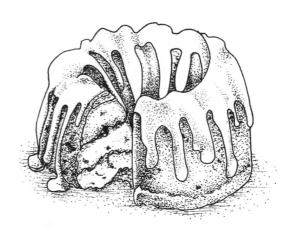

APPLE DATE COFFEE CAKE

Filling
1 ½ cups Granny Smith (or other baking apple), chopped
1 tablespoon flour
¼ teaspoon nutmeg
⅓ cup packed brown sugar
2 tablespoons butter or margarine
⅛ teaspoon salt
½ cup ground or finely chopped pecans

Cake
1 (18.25 ounce) yellow cake mix
1 (3.4 ounce) package vanilla flavor instant pudding mix
4 eggs
1 cup (8 ounces) sour cream
½ cup vegetable oil

Prepare filling: place all filling ingredients except pecans in a medium saucepan. Cook over medium heat, stirring constantly, until apples are tender (about 3 to 4 minutes). Stir in nuts, and let cool.

Prepare cake: preheat oven to 350°. In large bowl, combine cake mix, pudding mix, eggs, sour cream and oil. Beat on low speed to blend, then beat on medium for 2 minutes.

Spread ⅓ batter into greased and floured 12-cup capacity Bundt cake pan. Sprinkle half filling mixture evenly over. Spread another third of batter over filling, and sprinkle remaining filling on top. Spread remaining batter over.

(continued)

Bake for 45 to 50 minutes, or until cake tester comes out clean. Cool in pan for 10 minutes, then turn out onto serving platter. Sprinkle with powdered sugar, or if desired, drizzle Powdered Sugar Glaze over.

Powdered Sugar Glaze

¾ cup powdered sugar
½ teaspoon vanilla (clear)
3 teaspoons warm water

In small bowl, combine sugar and vanilla. Add water, a teaspoon at a time at a time, until icing reaches drizzling consistency.

Drizzle over cake, using a knife to spread more evenly on the top of cake, and let it run down the sides. (You need to work fast, because this icing hardens quickly.)

STRAWBERRY BUNDT CAKE

1 (8 ounce) package cream cheese, softened
⅓ cup sugar
4 eggs, divided
1 teaspoon lemon extract
1 (18.25 ounce) white cake mix
1 (10 ounce) container sweetened strawberries,
  drained, juice reserved
½ cup (4 ounces) sour cream
2 tablespoons vegetable oil
¼ cup powdered sugar, optional (for garnish)

Preheat oven to 350°. In small bowl, cream cheese with sugar, until well blended. Beat in 1 egg and lemon extract. Set aside.

In large bowl, combine cake mix, strawberry juice, remaining eggs, sour cream and oil. Beat on low speed to blend. Beat on medium speed for 2 minutes. Pour batter into greased and floured 12-cup capacity Bundt cake pan.

Pour cream cheese mixture over center of batter, avoiding sides of pan. Gently swirl mixture through batter with a knife, taking care not to over mix.

Bake for 40 to 50 minutes, or until cake tester comes out clean. Let cake cool in pan for 10 minutes, then turn out onto cooling rack. Dust with powdered sugar for decoration.

ORANGE BANANA BUNDT CAKE WITH BUTTERMILK GLAZE

1 (18.25 ounce) yellow cake mix
1 (8 ounce) container sour cream
½ cup vegetable oil
4 eggs
2 tablespoons orange zest (grated orange rind)
1 cup ripe mashed bananas

Preheat oven to 350°. In large bowl, combine cake mix, sour cream, oil, eggs, orange zest and bananas. Beat on low speed to blend, then beat on medium for 2 minutes.

Pour batter into greased and floured 12-cup capacity Bundt cake pan. Bake for 50 minutes, or until cake tester comes out clean. Cool in pan for 10 minutes, then turn out onto serving platter. Spoon Buttermilk Glaze over warm cake.

Buttermilk Glaze
½ cup sugar
¼ cup buttermilk
¼ cup (½ stick) butter or margarine
½ teaspoon vanilla
2 teaspoons corn syrup

Combine all ingredients in medium saucepan and bring to a simmer over medium heat. Cook for five minutes, stirring constantly. Remove from heat and let cool slightly.

Start making Buttermilk Glaze while the cake is baking (during the last 20 minutes or so). It will be ready for the cake when you remove it from the pan, and ready to eat that much sooner.

STRAWBERRY BANANA CAKE

1 (18.25 ounce) French vanilla cake mix
1 (3.4 oz) vanilla flavor instant pudding mix
4 eggs
1 cup mashed bananas
½ cup vegetable oil
1 (10 ounce) container sweetened strawberries in
    syrup, drained, reserve syrup

Preheat oven to 350°. In large bowl, combine cake mix,
pudding mix, eggs, bananas, oil and strawberry syrup.
Beat on low speed to blend, then beat on medium for 2
to 3 minutes, until batter is thoroughly blended.

Gently stir in strawberries, taking care not to
obliterate them. Pour batter into greased and floured
12-cup capacity Bundt cake pan. Bake for 45 to 50
minutes, or until cake tester comes out clean. Cool
cake in pan for 10 minutes, then turn out onto cooling
rack. When cool, spoon Strawberry Topping over.

Strawberry Topping
1 tablespoon cornstarch
2 tablespoons orange liqueur (or 1 teaspoon orange
    extract and 1 ½ tablespoons water)
2 cups fresh strawberries, sliced
½ cup sugar
¼ cup orange juice

Dissolve cornstarch in orange liqueur. Combine
strawberries, sugar and orange juice in small saucepan,
and cook over medium heat until strawberries are soft
(about 10 minutes). Stir in cornstarch mixture, and
continue to cook until thickened (about 4 minutes).
Remove from heat and cool.

RASPBERRY SOUR CREAM CAKE

1 (18.25 ounce) butter recipe golden cake mix
⅓ cup sugar
1 cup sour cream
½ cup vegetable oil
4 eggs
1 (10 ounce) container sweetened raspberries,
   drained, reserve ¼ cup syrup for glaze

Do not preheat oven. In large bowl, combine cake mix, sugar, sour cream, oil and eggs. Beat on low speed to blend, then beat on medium for 4 minutes.

Pour ⅔ of batter into greased and floured 12-cup capacity Bundt cake pan. Drop raspberries on top of batter, and top with remaining batter. Place in cold oven, and set temperature to 325°. Bake for 50 to 55 minutes, or until cake tester comes out clean.

Cool cake in pan for 10 minutes, then turn out onto cooling rack. When cool, spoon Raspberry Glaze over.

Raspberry Glaze
2 cups powdered sugar
¼ cup reserved raspberry syrup
¼ teaspoon lemon extract

Gradually stir raspberry syrup into powdered sugar, blending well after each addition. Stir in lemon extract.

FUZZY CATERPILLAR CAKE

1 (18.25 ounce) white cake mix
1 (3.4 ounce) package vanilla flavor instant pudding mix
1 ¼ cups milk
4 eggs
⅓ cup vegetable oil

Preheat oven to 350°. In large bowl, combine cake mix, pudding mix, milk, eggs and oil. Beat on low speed to blend, then beat on medium for 2 minutes. Pour batter into greased and floured 12-cup capacity Bundt cake pan. Bake for 50 to 55 minutes, or until cake tester comes out clean. Cool cake in pan for 10 minutes, then turn out onto cooling rack.

When cool, cut cake in half (so that you have 2 semi-circles). Place one cut side of one semicircle against cut side of other semicircle to make an "s" shape. Cut the corners off the front of the cake, to give the "head" a rounded shape. Frost cake with Boiled White Icing, and then sprinkle with colored coconut (see Garnish section below).

In order to make the caterpillar's "feet," cut gumdrops in half vertically, and space them evenly apart on either side of the cake. Place two chocolate chips, one on either side of the head, for "eyes."

(continued)

Boiled White Icing
2 egg whites
1 cup sugar
⅓ cup water
¼ teaspoon cream of tartar
Pinch salt
1 teaspoon clear vanilla

Place egg whites in large bowl. Set aside.

In medium saucepan, combine sugar, water, cream of tartar and salt. Bring to a boil, stirring frequently until sugar dissolves.

Remove from heat and slowly add to egg whites in bowl, beating constantly with mixer until stiff peaks form. Beat in vanilla. Frosting will be very light and fluffy.

Garnish
1 cup shredded coconut
4 drops liquid food color
14 gumdrops, cut in half vertically (for legs)
2 round candies or chocolate chips (for eyes)

In medium bowl, combine coconut and food color. Stir well until coconut is evenly colored.

GINGER CAKE

1 (18.25 ounce) butter recipe golden cake mix
⅓ cup sugar
1 cup sour cream
½ cup vegetable oil
4 eggs
1 teaspoon ground ginger
1 tablespoon flour
½ cup crystallized ginger, minced

 Preheat oven to 350°. In large bowl, combine cake mix, sugar, sour cream, vegetable oil, eggs and ground ginger. Beat on low speed to blend, then beat on medium for two minutes.

In separate bowl, combine flour with ginger; toss to coat. Stir gently into batter.

Pour batter into greased and floured 12-cup capacity Bundt cake pan. Bake for 50 to 55 minutes, or until cake tester comes out clean. Cool cake in pan for 10 minutes, then turn out onto cooling rack. Serve with whipped cream.

BLACK WALNUT CAKE

1 (18.25 ounce) box white cake mix
1 ⅓ cups milk
⅓ cup water
2 tablespoons vegetable oil
3 eggs
1 cup finely ground black walnuts

Preheat oven to 350°. In large bowl, combine cake mix, milk, water, vegetable oil and eggs. Beat on low speed to blend, then beat on medium for two minutes more. Stir in black walnuts until well blended.

Divide batter between 2 greased and floured 9" round cake pans, and bake for 30 minutes or until cake springs back when lightly touched. Let cakes cool in pans for 10 minutes, then turn onto cooling rack. Ice with maple frosting.

Maple Frosting
½ cup (1 stick) butter or margarine
½ cup packed light brown sugar
½ cup real maple syrup
¼ cup milk
2 to 2 ½ cups powdered sugar (divided)

Melt butter in a medium saucepan. Add the brown sugar and maple syrup, and bring to a boil. Boil for 2 minutes, stirring constantly. Add the milk, and bring back to a boil.

Stir in ¼ cup powdered sugar, remove from heat, and let cool to lukewarm temperature. Gradually beat in the remaining sugar until frosting is of spreading consistency.

101

MARBLED BANANA CHOCOLATE LAYER CAKE

1 (18.25 ounce) white cake mix
1 cup milk
3 eggs
⅓ cup vegetable oil
¼ cup sugar
½ cup mashed bananas
1 cup semi-sweet chocolate chips, melted

Preheat oven to 350°. In large bowl, combine cake mix, milk, eggs, oil and sugar. Beat on low speed to blend, then beat on medium for 2 minutes.

Remove 2 cups of batter to a medium bowl and set aside. Add bananas to remaining batter in large bowl, and beat for another 30 seconds or so until blended.

Stir melted chocolate into reserved batter and mix until thoroughly blended.

Divide banana batter evenly between 2 greased and floured round cake pans. Drop chocolate batter by large spoonfuls evenly over banana batter in both pans. Use a butter knife or tip of icing spatula to swirl chocolate batter through banana batter, taking care not to over mix.

Bake for 30 minutes, or until cake tester comes out clean. Let cakes cool in pans for 10 minutes, then turn onto cooling rack. Ice with Chocolate Fudge Icing.

(continued)

Chocolate Fudge Icing
½ cup (1 stick) butter or margarine
2 tablespoons cocoa powder
3 tablespoons buttermilk
1 teaspoon vanilla
4 cups powdered sugar

🥣 Melt butter in medium saucepan over medium-high heat.

🥣 Add cocoa powder and buttermilk. Bring to a boil, stirring constantly. Remove from heat.

🥣 Add vanilla and then sugar, one cup at a time, beating after each addition. Immediately frost cake, as icing starts to harden quickly.

OATMEAL SPICE CAKE
WITH BROWN SUGAR FROSTING

1 ¼ cups water
1 cup quick-cooking oats
1 (18.25 ounce) spice cake mix
4 eggs
⅓ cup vegetable oil
½ cup milk

Preheat oven to 350°. Boil water, and combine with oats in medium bowl; stir well and set aside to cool slightly.

In large bowl, combine cake mix, eggs, oil and milk. Beat on low speed to blend, then beat on medium speed for 2 minutes. Add the cooled oatmeal and beat for 1 minute more.

Divide batter between 2 greased and floured round cake pans. Bake for 30 to 35 minutes, or until cakes test done. When cool, frost with Brown Sugar Frosting.

(continued)

Brown Sugar Frosting

½ cup (1 stick) butter or
  margarine
1 ½ cups packed dark brown sugar
½ cup milk
3 ½ cups powdered sugar
1 teaspoon vanilla

In medium saucepan, melt butter and brown sugar. Bring to a boil, stirring constantly, and slowly add milk.

Bring mixture back to a boil, and boil for 2 minutes. Remove from heat and cool.

Stir in powdered sugar and vanilla. Beat until smooth and of spreading consistency.

BLACKBERRY JAM CAKE
WITH CREAM CHEESE FROSTING

1 (18.25 ounce) white cake mix
3 eggs
⅓ cup vegetable oil
½ cup seedless blackberry jam (plus additional ⅓
   cup for filling, if desired)
1 cup buttermilk
½ teaspoon cinnamon
½ teaspoon allspice
¼ teaspoon nutmeg

Preheat oven to 350°. In large bowl, combine all
ingredients and beat on low speed until blended.
Beat on medium to high speed for 2 minutes, then
divide batter between 2 greased and floured round
cake pans.

Bake for 25 to 30 minutes, or until cakes test done.
Let cool, and frost with Cream Cheese Icing. If you
want to fill the layers with jam, read the instructions
for using jam filling on next page.

(continued)

Cream Cheese Icing
½ cup (1 stick) butter or margarine
1 (8 ounce) package cream cheese, softened
1 tablespoon milk or half-and-half
1 teaspoon vanilla
1 (1 lb.) box powdered sugar

In medium bowl, cream butter and cheese until light and fluffy. Beat in milk and vanilla; add powdered sugar, two cups at a time, blending well after each addition, until icing is smooth.

Using Jam Filling
A jam filling really enhances the flavor. In order to keep it from seeping out the sides and discoloring the icing, take some icing on the lip of a knife and spread it in a ring ½" from the edge of the cake layer. Try to make it thick, say ¼" inch deep. Then just spread the jam within this icing ring, place the second cake layer on top and frost the top and sides of the cake.

AUTUMN SPICE CAKE

1 (18.25 ounce) spice cake mix
1 (1 lb.) can pumpkin
3 eggs
⅓ cup orange juice (or water)
1 teaspoon cinnamon

Preheat oven to 350°. Combine all ingredients and beat on low speed for 30 seconds to blend. Then beat on high speed for two minutes.

Divide batter between two greased and floured round cake pans, and bake for 25 or 30 minutes, or until the cakes test done.

Cool and frost with Maple Cream Cheese frosting.

(continued)

Maple Cream Cheese Frosting
¼ cup (½ stick) butter
1 (8 ounce) package cream cheese, softened
¼ cup maple syrup (real maple syrup if possible)
4 cups powdered sugar

With mixer on low, blend butter and cream cheese. Add maple syrup and mix well.

Slowly add powdered sugar, beating after each addition, until well blended.

The icing for this really enhances the pumpkin and spice flavors. For the best flavor, I use real maple syrup. Its intense flavor can't be matched by the artificial maple syrups.

BANANA LAYER CAKE
WITH BUTTER PECAN FROSTING

1 (18.25 ounce) yellow cake mix
3 eggs
⅓ cup vegetable oil
½ cup packed light brown sugar
1 cup milk
1 cup mashed ripe bananas, (about 2 ½ medium
   bananas)
1 cup coarsely chopped pecans, toasted (optional)

Preheat oven to 350°. In large bowl, combine cake
mix, eggs, oil, sugar and milk. Beat on low speed to
blend, then beat on medium for 2 minutes.

Add bananas and beat for 1 more minute on medium
speed. If desired, stir in pecans.

Divide batter between 2 greased and floured round
cake pans.

Bake for 30 to 35 minutes, or until cake tester
comes out clean.

Cool and frost with Butter Pecan Frosting.

(continued)

Butter Pecan Frosting

½ cup (1 stick) butter or margarine
6 cups powdered sugar
4 tablespoons light cream
1 teaspoon vanilla
½ teaspoon butter flavoring
1 cup chopped pecans, toasted

In large bowl, cream butter, 2 cups powdered sugar, cream, vanilla and butter flavoring until smooth.

Add remaining powdered sugar in several additions, mixing well after each addition. Stir in pecans.

Toasting Pecans

Toast the pecans by placing them on a cookie sheet in a 300° oven for 8 to 10 minutes. Remove them when they become lightly browned. (Watch closely to be sure they don't burn.)

ZUCCHINI CAKE WITH LEMON CREAM CHEESE FROSTING

1 (18.25 ounce) spice cake mix
1 teaspoon cinnamon
½ teaspoon nutmeg
3 eggs
⅓ cup vegetable oil
2 teaspoons fresh lemon juice
¼ cup orange juice
¼ cup honey
2 cups finely grated zucchini
½ cup coarsely chopped walnuts (optional)

Preheat oven to 350°. In large bowl, combine cake mix, cinnamon and nutmeg. Add eggs, oil, lemon juice, orange juice and honey. Mix on low speed to blend, then beat on medium for 2 minutes.

Stir in zucchini (and walnuts, if desired).

Divide batter between 2 greased and floured round cake pans. Bake for 30 to 35 minutes, or until cakes test done. Cool and frost with Lemon Cream Cheese Frosting.

(continued)

Lemon Cream Cheese Frosting
1 (8 ounce) package cream cheese, softened
½ cup (1 stick) butter or margarine, softened
1 teaspoon lemon extract
1 teaspoon vanilla
4 ½ to 5 cups powdered sugar
½ cup chopped pecans, toasted*

In medium bowl, mix cream cheese, butter, lemon extract and vanilla until thoroughly blended.

Add powdered sugar slowly, mixing well after each addition, until mixture reaches spreading consistency. Stir in pecans.

See tip on Toasting Pecans on page 111.

COOKIES AND CREAM LAYER CAKE

1 (18.25 ounces) white cake mix
½ cup (4 ounces) sour cream
¾ cup milk
3 egg whites
2 tablespoons vegetable oil
2 cups crushed chocolate sandwich cookies, like
    Oreos, divided (you'll need about 18)

Preheat oven to 350°. In large mixing bowl, combine
cake mix, sour cream, milk, egg whites and oil. Beat
on low speed to blend, then beat on medium for 2 to
3 minutes.

Stir 1 ½ cups crushed cookies into batter. Divide
batter between 2 greased and floured round cake
pans.

Bake for 30 to 35 minutes, or until cake tester comes
out clean. Cool and frost with White Frosting, then
sprinkle remaining ½ cup of crushed cookies on top
of cake for decoration.

(continued)

White Frosting
½ cup milk
1 tablespoon cornstarch
½ cup vegetable shortening
4 cups powdered sugar, divided
1 ½ teaspoons vanilla

Blend milk and cornstarch. Place in small saucepan and cook over low heat, stirring constantly, until mixture is thickened. Remove from heat and let cool.

In medium bowl, cream shortening with 1 cup powdered sugar until mixture is light and fluffy. Add milk mixture and blend well.

Stir in vanilla, and then remaining powdered sugar 1 cup at a time, mixing well after each addition, until frosting reaches spreading consistency.

To crush the cookies for this cake, I use a sealable plastic bag. Place the cookies in the bag, and use a rolling pin to crush them by gently pounding them or rolling over them. Be careful not to pulverize the cookies; I like to have them coarsely broken, not smashed beyond recognition.

DEVIL'S FOOD CREAM CHEESE CAKE

  1 (8 ounce) package cream cheese, softened
  ⅓ cup sugar
  4 eggs, divided
  1 teaspoon vanilla
  1 (18.25 ounce) devil's food cake mix
  1 cup buttermilk
  ⅓ cup vegetable oil

Preheat oven to 350°. In small bowl, cream cheese with sugar until blended. Beat in 1 egg and vanilla until mixture is light and fluffy.

In large bowl, combine cake mix with buttermilk, oil and remaining eggs. Beat on low speed to blend, then beat on medium for 2 minutes.

Divide batter between 2 greased and floured round cake pans. Divide cream cheese mixture evenly between the cakes, dropping by spoonsful onto batter. Gently swirl it with knife or spatula to create a marbled effect. Bake for 30 to 35 minutes, or until cake tester comes out clean. Cool cakes and frost with Fudge Frosting.

Fudge Frosting
  4 ounces unsweetened chocolate, melted
  ½ cup (1 stick) butter or margarine, melted
  ½ cup whipping cream
  1 (1 pound) box powdered sugar
  2 teaspoons vanilla

Combine chocolate and butter; stir until well blended. In medium bowl, stir whipping cream into powdered sugar, then stir in vanilla. Add chocolate mixture and beat until completely mixed. If frosting is too thin, place bowl in larger bowl of ice water and continue to beat until mixture reaches frosting consistency.

RED VELVET CAKE

1 (18.25 ounce) white cake mix
1 (3.4 ounce) vanilla flavor instant pudding mix
3 tablespoons cocoa
4 eggs
1 cup milk
½ cup vegetable oil
1 ounce red food coloring

Preheat oven to 350°. In large bowl, combine all ingredients. Beat on low speed to blend, then beat on medium speed for 4 minutes.

Divide batter between 3 greased and floured round cake pans. Bake for 25 to 30 minutes, or until cake tester comes out clean. Cool and frost with Cream Cheese Icing.

Cream Cheese Icing
¾ cup (1 ½ sticks) butter or margarine, softened
1 ½ (8 ounce) packages cream cheese, softened
1 ½ teaspoons vanilla
1 ½ teaspoons almond extract
1 ½ - 2 (1 pound) boxes powdered sugar

Cream butter and cream cheese until blended.

Add vanilla and almond extract; gradually add powdered sugar, blending well after each addition.

CHERRY CAKE

1 (18.25 ounce) white cake mix
1 ⅓ cups milk
2 tablespoons vegetable oil
3 egg whites
¾ cup white chocolate chips, melted
¾ cup maraschino cherries, well drained and
    coarsely chopped

Preheat oven to 350°. In large bowl, combine cake
mix, milk, oil, egg whites and white chocolate. Beat
on low speed to blend, then beat on medium for 3
minutes. Gently stir in cherries.

Divide batter between 2 greased and floured round
cake pans. Bake for 30 to 35 minutes, or until cake
tester comes out clean. Cool and frost with Cherry
Frosting.

Cherry Frosting
⅓ cup milk
3 tablespoons butter or margarine, softened
5 to 6 cups powdered sugar
2 tablespoons maraschino cherry juice
6 maraschino cherries, chopped

In medium bowl, combine milk, butter and 1 cup
powdered sugar. Beat in cherry juice and remaining
powdered sugar a little at a time. Fold in chopped
cherries.

WATERMELON CAKE WITH LIME FROSTING

1 (3.0 ounce) package watermelon flavor gelatin
1 cup warm water
1 (18.25 ounce) white cake mix
4 eggs
½ cup vegetable oil
Several drops of red food coloring (optional)

Preheat oven to 350°. In large bowl, stir gelatin into water until dissolved. Add cake mix, eggs and oil. (At this point, you can add several drops of red food coloring, if desired, to color the batter a deeper pink or red.) Blend on low speed to moisten, then beat on medium for 2 minutes.

Divide batter between 2 greased and floured round cake pans. Bake for 30 minutes, or until cake tester comes out clean. Cool and frost with Lime Frosting.

Lime Frosting
½ cup (1 stick) butter or margarine, softened
3 to 3 ½ cups powdered sugar
4 tablespoons fresh lime juice
1 teaspoon lime zest (grated lime rind)
1 teaspoon vanilla (clear)
Several drops of green food coloring (optional)

In medium bowl, cream butter with 1 cup powdered sugar. Add lime juice, zest and vanilla. Blend well. Gradually add remaining powdered sugar, beating well after each addition, until frosting reaches spreading consistency. (If desired, add a few drops of green food coloring.)

ALMOND CHERRY TORTE

1 (18.25 ounce) white cake mix
3 eggs
1 ⅓ cups buttermilk
3 tablespoons vegetable oil
2 teaspoons almond extract
1 tablespoon flour
1 cup sliced almonds

Preheat oven to 350°. In large bowl, combine cake mix, eggs, buttermilk, oil and almond extract. Beat on low speed to blend, then beat on medium for two minutes.

In small bowl, coat almonds with flour, then stir into batter. Divide batter between 2 greased and floured round cake pans. Bake for 30 to 35 minutes, or until cake tester comes out clean. Cool and frost with Cherry Filling and Icing.

Cherry Filling and Icing
2 ½ cups heavy whipping cream
3 tablespoons powdered sugar
2 cups cherry preserves, divided

In medium bowl, beat whipping cream on high speed until soft peaks form. Add powdered sugar and continue to beat until stiff. Fold in 1 cup cherry preserves.

Slice each cake layer in half. Spread ⅓ whip cream filling on bottom cake layer. Top with second cake layer and spread with 1 cup remaining cherry preserves. Top with third cake layer and spread ⅓ whip cream filling over. Top with fourth cake layer. Spread remaining whip cream filling over top and sides. Refrigerate until ready to serve.

APRICOT TORTE

1 (18.25 ounce) butter recipe golden cake mix
½ cup (1 stick) butter or margarine, softened
3 eggs
⅔ cup reserved apricot syrup from 1 (16 ounce) can
   apricot halves (see Filling recipe below)

Preheat oven to 350°. In large bowl, combine cake
mix, butter, eggs and apricot syrup. Beat on low
speed to blend, then beat on medium for 3 minutes.

Divide batter between 2 greased and floured round
cake pans. Bake for 30 minutes, or until cake tester
comes out clean. Let cool. Slice each layer
horizontally, then fill and frost with Filling and
Frosting. Keep cake refrigerated.

Filling and Frosting
1 (8 ounce) package cream cheese, softened
1 (14 ounce) can sweetened condensed milk
¼ cup fresh lemon juice
1 (12 ounce) container frozen whipped topping,
   thawed
1 (16 ounce) can apricot halves, drained, chopped
   (reserve ⅔ cup syrup)

In large bowl, combine cream cheese and condensed
milk. Beat on low to medium speed until smooth.
Stir in lemon juice, then whipped topping. Blend
well. Fold in chopped apricots.

LUSCIOUS ORANGE TORTE

1 (3 ounce) package orange flavor instant gelatin
1 cup orange juice
1 (18.25 ounce) yellow cake mix
½ cup oil
3 eggs

Preheat oven to 350°. Stir gelatin into orange juice until dissolved. In large bowl, combine orange juice-gelatin mixture with cake mix, oil and eggs. Beat on low speed to blend, then beat on medium for 3 minutes. Divide batter between 2 greased and floured round cake pans. Bake for 30 minutes, or until cake tester comes out clean.

Let cakes cool slightly in pan, then poke holes ½" apart over entire surface of each and spoon Orange Glaze evenly over, allowing glaze to be absorbed. Let cakes sit undisturbed for about an hour, then assemble.

Cut each layer in half. Fill the first layer with half of filling. Top with second layer and cover with some frosting. Place third layer on top, and fill with remaining filling. Top with fourth layer. Frost cake top and sides with remaining frosting. (Keep refrigerated.)

Orange Glaze
2 cups powdered sugar
⅔ cup orange juice
Zest (grated rind) of one orange

(continued)

In small bowl, gradually whisk orange juice into powdered sugar. Whisk in orange zest. (If not using immediately, stir again just before use, as the zest rises to the top of the glaze and needs to be incorporated before you pour it over the cake.)

Filling
1 (14 ounce) can sweetened condensed milk
$\frac{1}{3}$ cup fresh lemon juice
4 ounces frozen whipped topping, thawed

In medium bowl, combine condensed milk and lemon juice; stir until well blended. Fold in whipped topping. Refrigerate until use.

Frosting
1 (20 ounce) can crushed pineapple, with juice
1 (3.4 ounce) vanilla flavor instant pudding mix
1 (8 ounce) container frozen whipped topping, thawed

In large bowl, combine pineapple (with juice) and pudding mix. Stir well. Fold in whipped topping.

BANANA SPLIT TORTE

This cake is a cinch to put together—the whipped cream only takes a few minutes to make, and with no frosting to prepare, once the cake has cooled, you can quickly create a pretty dessert with hardly any effort.

1 (18.25 ounce) white cake mix
1 ⅓ cups milk
¼ cup vegetable oil
3 eggs
2 teaspoons butter flavoring
1 cup mashed bananas
1 cup heavy whipping cream
2 tablespoons powdered sugar
1 cup fresh sliced strawberries
1 (8 ounce) can crushed pineapple, drained
1 (12 ounce) jar fudge ice cream topping
¼ cup chopped nuts (for garnish)

Preheat oven to 350°. In large bowl, combine cake mix, milk, oil, eggs, butter flavoring and bananas. Beat on low speed to blend, then beat on medium for 2 minutes. Divide batter between 2 greased and floured round cake pans. Bake for 30 minutes, or until cake tester comes out clean. Cool.

While cake is baking (or cooling), prepare the fillings and refrigerate until cake is cooled and ready for assembly: Beat whipping cream with powdered sugar until stiff peaks form. Divide in half. Fold the strawberries into one half of whipped cream. Fold pineapple into the other.

(continued)

To assemble cake:

Warm the fudge topping slightly to make it easier to work with. (You can warm it in a small saucepan over low heat, or in the microwave at half power, stirring every 30 seconds or so to keep it from getting too hot.)

Split each cake layer horizontally. Place the bottom of one layer on serving plate and top with strawberry cream, spreading cream evenly over surface. Place second cake layer on top, and spoon half the fudge topping over, letting it drip down the sides of bottom layer.

Place a third layer on top, and spread pineapple cream evenly over. Top with fourth layer, and spoon remaining fudge topping over, covering entire surface and letting it drip down the sides. Sprinkle nuts over fudge.

Keep cake refrigerated until ready to serve.

DEEP DARK CHOCOLATE ORANGE TORTE

1 (18.25 ounce) devil's food cake mix
3 eggs
⅓ cup vegetable oil
1 ⅓ cups buttermilk
3 teaspoons orange extract

Preheat oven to 350°. In large bowl, combine cake mix, eggs, oil, buttermilk and orange extract. Beat on low speed to blend, then beat on medium for 2 minutes.

Divide batter between 2 greased and floured round cake pans, and bake for 30 to 35 minutes, or until cake tester comes out clean. Cool cakes and slice each layer in half.

Fill first layer with half of Orange Filling, place second layer on top, and frost with some Chocolate Frosting. Top with third layer and fill with remaining Orange Filling. Place fourth layer on top and frost top and sides with remaining Chocolate Frosting.

Orange Filling
1 cup sugar
4 tablespoons cornstarch
3 teaspoons orange zest (grated orange peel)
½ teaspoon salt
1 ½ cups orange juice
½ cup water
4 slightly beaten egg yolks
4 tablespoons butter or margarine

(continued)

🥄 In medium saucepan, combine sugar, cornstarch, orange zest and salt. Gradually whisk in orange juice, water and egg yolks. Blend well, and bring to a simmer, whisking mixture frequently.

🥄 Cook over medium heat until thickened. Remove from heat. Stir in butter until melted. Cool slightly.

Chocolate Frosting

⅓ cup (5 ⅓ tablespoons) butter or margarine
⅔ cup unsweetened cocoa powder
1 teaspoon vanilla
⅓ cup milk
3 cups powdered sugar

🥄 In medium saucepan, melt butter over medium heat; add cocoa powder, stirring until well-blended and mixture starts to boil. Remove from heat.

🥄 Add vanilla and half of milk, stirring until well blended. Stir in 1 cup of powdered sugar. Stir in remaining milk, then add remaining powdered sugar, 1 cup at a time, beating until frosting is smooth.

If you're short on time, forget the filling and just frost the cake without splitting the layers. It's just as delicious.

PINEAPPLE TORTE

1 (18.25 ounce) white cake mix
½ cup reserved pineapple juice (see Pineapple Filling
  below)
3 eggs
¼ cup vegetable oil
¾ cup milk

Preheat oven to 350°. In large bowl, combine cake
mix, ½ cup pineapple juice, eggs, oil and milk. Beat
on low speed to blend, then on medium speed for 3
minutes. Divide batter between 2 greased and
floured round cake pans, and bake for 25 to 30
minutes, or until cake tests done. Cool cakes and
cut each layer in half.

Assemble cake by filling first layer with half of the
pineapple filling, placing second layer on top and
filling with about 1 cup of 7 Minute Frosting. Place
third layer on top and fill with remaining pineapple
filling. Top with fourth cake layer and frost cake top
and sides with remaining frosting.

Pineapple Filling
1 cup sugar
4 tablespoons flour
1 (20 ounce) can crushed pineapple and juice (½ cup
  juice reserved separately)
2 eggs, beaten
2 tablespoons fresh lemon juice
1 tablespoon butter or margarine
1 teaspoon vanilla

(continued)

Combine sugar and flour and place in medium saucepan. Add remaining ingredients, and cook over medium heat, stirring constantly until mixture thickens (about 3 to 4 minutes). Remove from heat and let cool.

7 Minute Frosting

1 ½ cups sugar
¼ cup, plus 1 tablespoon water
2 egg whites
1 tablespoon light corn syrup
Pinch of salt
1 teaspoon vanilla (colorless—to avoid discoloring the icing)

Combine sugar, water, egg whites, corn syrup and salt in top of double boiler; beat constantly on high speed over boiling water for 7 minutes. Remove from heat and add vanilla. Continue beating until stiff peaks form (about 4 more minutes) and frosting reaches spreading consistency.

I like to add a little yellow food coloring to the frosting when I add the vanilla in order to make the icing color match the yellow cake and filling.

If you're not in the mood to make the filling and frosting, just forget the filling, and frost the cake layers with the 7 minute frosting.

KAHLUA MOUSSE TORTE
(Otherwise known as "Nana's Midnight Snack Cake")

Cake
1 (18.25 ounce) devil's food cake mix
¾ cup Kahlua
½ cup strong coffee
3 eggs
½ cup vegetable oil

Preheat oven to 350°. In large mixing bowl, combine cake mix, Kahlua, coffee, eggs and oil. Beat on low speed to blend, then beat on medium for 2 minutes more.

Divide batter evenly between 2 greased and floured round baking pans. Bake for 30 to 35 minutes, or until cakes test done. Cool completely.

To assemble cake, slice each cake layer in half horizontally and top first layer with one third of Chocolate Mousse Filling. Top with second cake layer and pour half of Chocolate Glaze over, letting it run down sides of cake. At this point, if possible, refrigerate this layer to set the chocolate and mousse (for about an hour). Put another third of mousse over chocolate, and top with third cake layer. Cover third layer with remaining mousse, and put fourth cake layer on top. Spoon remaining chocolate glaze over, letting some of it drip over cake edges. Refrigerate immediately.

Chocolate Mousse Filling
4 egg yolks
¼ cup sugar
2 ½ cups heavy whipping cream, divided
1 cup semi-sweet chocolate chips

(continued)

In small bowl, beat egg yolks on high speed until thick (about 3 minutes). Gradually beat in sugar.

In medium saucepan, heat 1 cup whipping cream over medium heat just until hot (do not boil). Slowly stir some of the heated whipping cream into the egg and sugar mixture, then stir it back into the cream in the saucepan. Cook over low heat for 5 minutes, stirring constantly, until mixture is thickened. (Do not bring to a boil.)

Add chocolate chips, and stir until melted. Remove from heat. Cover and refrigerate until chilled (about 1 ½ hours).

Beat remaining 1 ½ cups whipping cream on high speed until stiff peaks form. Gently fold chilled chocolate mixture into whipped cream until incorporated.

Chocolate Glaze
½ cup heavy whipping cream
1 cup semi-sweet chocolate chips

In small saucepan, heat whipping cream and chocolate over medium heat until chocolate is melted and mixture is smooth (do not boil). Remove from heat and let cool to room temperature.

I decided to add this to the cookbook because my two sisters (Tania and Sabrina) said they needed a recipe for their "chocolate fix"! Tania, who goes by "Nana" to her nephews, is a big midnight snacker. This cake was designed to be the perfect late-night snack.

CHOCOLATE BOURBON CAKE
WITH PRALINE CREAM

1 (18.25 ounce) Swiss chocolate cake mix
1 (3.8 ounce) chocolate flavor instant pudding mix
½ cup bourbon
½ cup vegetable oil
½ cup buttermilk
4 eggs
1 cup chopped pecans, toasted
¼ cup caramel sauce (optional)

Preheat oven to 350°. In large bowl, combine cake mix, pudding mix, bourbon, oil, buttermilk and eggs. Beat on low speed to blend, then beat on medium speed for 2 minutes. Stop after 1 minute to scrape bowl.

Stir in pecans, and divide batter between 3 greased and floured round cake pans. Bake for 20 to 25 minutes, or until cake tester comes out clean.

When cool, fill each layer with ⅓ praline cream mixture and spreading remaining ⅓ of mixture on top layer. If desired, drizzle caramel sauce over top and let it drip down cake sides.

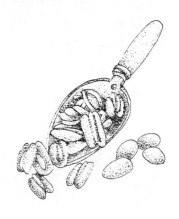

(continued)

Praline Cream Mixture
2 cups heavy whipping cream
2 tablespoons powdered sugar
⅓ cup caramel sauce (see recipe on page 199)

In medium bowl, combine whipping cream and powdered sugar. Beat on high speed with mixer until stiff peaks form. Fold in caramel sauce until well blended.

For added effect, sprinkle candied pecan halves over the top. See Special Touches on page 16. They are easy to make, and only take a little extra time, but they sure will make the cake look extra delicious. (You may also want to make them from time to time just for a snack. They keep for days in an airtight container.)

ORANGE MERINGUE TORTE
WITH APRICOT FILLING

Topping your cakes with meringue adds texture and elegance with very little effort. The combination of cake, meringue, and filling add up to one impressive, delicious dessert.

1 (18.25 ounce) yellow cake mix
1 (3 ounce) package orange flavor gelatin
4 eggs, separated
1 cup orange juice
⅓ cup vegetable oil
Pinch salt
1 cup sugar
1 teaspoon vanilla

Preheat oven to 350°. In large bowl combine cake mix, gelatin, egg yolks, orange juice and oil. Beat on low speed to blend, then beat on medium for 3 minutes. Divide batter between 2 greased and floured round cake pans. Set aside while you prepare meringue topping.

(continued)

In medium bowl, beat egg whites and salt on high speed until soft peaks form. Add sugar in several additions, beating well after each addition. Add vanilla and beat until mixture is stiff and glossy. Spread the meringue evenly over the cake batter in each pan, smoothing the surface and spreading it to the edges of the cake pans.

Bake for 35 minutes, or until meringue is lightly browned and cake tester comes out clean. Let cakes cool in pans for 10 minutes, then carefully remove each layer to a cooling rack, right side up. (To remove cakes from pans, you can place a flat plate or your hand over the meringue side, turn the pan upside down, and then gently place cake right side up on rack.) The meringue will crack a little, which is O.K.

When well cooled, spread one layer with half of Apricot Filling and place other layer on top. Frost sides of cake with remaining half of filling (leaving top meringue layer exposed).

Apricot Filling
1 ½ cups heavy whipping cream
2 tablespoons powdered sugar
¾ cup apricot preserves

In medium bowl, beat whipping cream until soft peaks form, then add powdered sugar and beat until stiff. Fold in apricot preserves.

I love being able to use a cake mix to make the following recipes. Pastries of this sort always looked so complicated to me, and I found myself hesitating before trying to make them. When I started making them with the cake mixes, I realized how easy they are!

Yes, they take a little longer than a cake, because once you mix the dough, you have to wait for it to rise, then work it, make your pastry, and then let it rise again, but the whole process can be done within a couple of hours. And then you have hot, fresh baked goods that look like you went to the bakery.

Another great thing about using a mix is the flavor. The dough has a sweeter taste to it, which I like, and it's very moist. One of my biggest complaints about buying cinnamon rolls or pastry at the store is that it's so often a little dry—too "bready." These aren't!

These are great "Saturday morning" recipes. Try preparing as much as you can the night before, by getting out the non-perishable ingredients and utensils you'll need, then put it together first thing in the morning. (After you've had that first cup of coffee of course.)

CHOCOLATE-FILLED CUPCAKES

1 (18.25 ounce) devil's food cake mix
1 ⅓ cups buttermilk
4 eggs, divided
⅓ cup vegetable oil
1 cup mini semi-sweet chocolate chips, divided
1 (8 ounce) package cream cheese, softened
½ cup sugar

Preheat oven to 350°. In large bowl, combine cake mix, buttermilk, 3 eggs and oil. Beat on low speed to blend, then beat on medium for 2 minutes. Stir ½ cup chocolate chips into batter and set aside.

In medium bowl, beat cream cheese, sugar and remaining egg until mixture is smooth. Melt remaining ½ cup chocolate chips and add to cheese mixture. Beat until well blended.

Prepare 24 muffin pans, by either greasing and flouring or using paper baking cups. Fill each cup ½ full with batter. Drop a tablespoon of chocolate cheese mixture in center, and spoon remaining batter evenly over. Bake for 25 minutes.

COLOSSAL PETITS FOURS

I have always loved petits fours. I don't know what it is about the tiny little cakes that I like so much—their attractive little colorful decorations, the jam sandwiched between the tasty cake or the rich satisfying taste of icing, cake and jam in every bite-sized morsel.

Here's a larger version made with oversized cookie cutters in fun holiday and specialty shapes.

Cake
1 (18.25 ounce) white cake mix
1 ⅓ cups buttermilk
3 eggs
¼ cup vegetable oil
1 teaspoon almond extract
Jam for filling

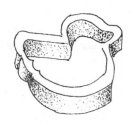

Preheat oven to 350°. In large bowl, combine cake mix, buttermilk, eggs, oil, and almond extract.

Beat on low speed to blend, then beat on medium for 2 minutes.

Pour batter into greased and floured jelly roll pan and bake for 20 to 25 minutes, or until cake tester comes out clean.

Turn out onto cooling rack until cool, then place on flat surface.

Cut shapes with cookie cutters (your cutters should be about 1½ to 2 inches tall). Slice in half horizontally and fill with thin layer of jam.

(continued)

🥣 Place cakes back on cooling rack and put a piece of waxed paper beneath rack to catch icing drips.

🥣 Spoon glaze over cakes, letting it run down the sides to cover the cakes as much as possible. If you'd like, while glaze is still wet, sprinkle colored sugar or candy jimmies over for decoration.

White Chocolate Glaze
½ cup milk
¾ cup white chocolate chips
4 cups powdered sugar

🥣 In medium saucepan, heat milk and white chocolate chips over low heat, stirring constantly until chips are melted. Remove from heat.

🥣 Gradually stir in powdered sugar, beating as you add it, until mixture is smooth. (If desired, tint the glaze by adding a few drops of food coloring, one drop at a time, stirring after each addition until glaze reaches the color you want.)

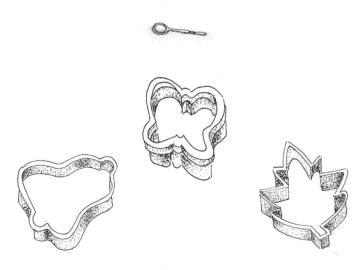

CINNAMON ROLLS

1 (18.25 ounce) yellow cake mix
5 to 5 ½ cups flour, divided
2 (.25 ounce) packages dry yeast
2 ½ cups warm (110°F) water, divided
½ cup (1 stick) butter or margarine, softened
1 cup packed brown sugar
4 teaspoons cinnamon
1 cup finely chopped pecans

In large bowl, combine cake mix and 3 cups flour; stir to thoroughly mix.

In medium bowl, stir yeast into ½ cup warm water. Add to cake and flour mixture. Add remaining 2 cups warm water, and mix into dough. Add remaining 2 to 2 ½ cups flour to make dough pliable. (You'll want the dough to be workable, not sticky.) If necessary, add a little more flour to get the consistency right. Cover and let rise until doubled in size (about an hour)*.

In small bowl, mix butter, sugar, cinnamon, and pecans.

Divide dough in half. Roll one half into a rectangle about ½" thick. Spread half of sugar mixture evenly over dough, and roll dough from the long side. Cut into ½" thick slices, and place on greased cookie sheet, cut side down with sides touching. Repeat with other half of dough.

(continued)

 Cover rolls and set aside to let rise again until doubled in size. Bake at 375° for 10 to 15 minutes. Remove from oven and drizzle with Powdered Sugar Icing.

Powdered Sugar Icing
2 cups powdered sugar
1 teaspoon vanilla (clear)
3 tablespoons warm water

 In small bowl, combine above ingredients and stir until well blended and of drizzling consistency.

See note on page 143 on Helping Dough Rise.

CREAM CHEESE FILLED COFFEE CAKE ROLLS

Pastry dough
2 (.25 ounce) packages dry yeast
1 teaspoon sugar
2 ½ cups warm water (110° F), divided
1 (18.25 ounce) yellow cake mix
4 ½ cups flour, divided

Filling
1 (8 ounce) package cream cheese, softened
¼ cup sugar
1 egg yolk (reserve the white)
1 tablespoon sour cream
½ teaspoon vanilla
½ cup raisins
½ cup ground walnuts

Topping
1 egg white
2 tablespoons sugar
¼ cup chopped walnuts

Prepare dough: in small bowl, stir yeast and sugar into ½ cup water. Let sit for 10 minutes, until foamy.

In large bowl, combine cake mix and flour. Stir in water and yeast mixture, plus remaining 2 cups water. Mix well. Cover and let rise in warm location until doubled in size (about 1 hour).

Prepare the filling: cream the cheese and sugar until light and fluffy. Add egg yolk, sour cream, and vanilla. Blend well. Stir in raisins and walnuts. Set aside.

(continued)

Roll out dough on heavily floured surface into rectangle about 18" by 16". Spread filling evenly over dough.

Roll dough jelly-roll fashion starting from longest side. Cut roll in half, and place the 2 rolls seam-side down on greased cookie sheet.

Cut slashes 2" apart in tops of rolls. Cover loosely with plastic wrap, and set aside to rise again until doubled in size.

Preheat oven to 350°. Brush tops of rolls with egg white. Sprinkle 1 tablespoon sugar, then half the walnuts over each roll. Bake for 25 to 30 minutes, until well browned.

Helping Dough Rise

To provide a good environment for rising dough and to hasten the process, you can use the following method. Take a small or medium pan of boiling water and place it on the bottom rack of your oven, then place the covered dough on the rack above.

The warmth from the hot water helps the dough rise, while keeping the air around it moist, preventing it from drying out. (It also provides a place to stash the bowl out of sight and out of your way, so you can clean up the mess you made making it!)

STICKY BUNS

Try these for a brunch or morning get together. Soft and fluffy, topped with caramel-coated pecans, they look and taste like they came straight from the bakery!

2 (.25 ounce) packages dry yeast
2 ½ cups warm water (110° F)
1 (18.25 ounce) yellow cake mix
4 cups flour
½ cup butter or margarine, divided
2 tablespoons sugar
1 teaspoon cinnamon
¼ cup light corn syrup
¼ cup packed brown sugar
2 cups pecan halves

Dissolve yeast in water, and let rest for 10 minutes. In a large bowl, combine cake mix and flour. Stir in water and yeast mixture. Blend well. Cover bowl and let rise in warm place until doubled in volume (about an hour).

Roll dough on a floured work surface into a rectangle about a ¼" thick (about 12" x 24" in diameter). Melt ¼ cup butter, and spread over dough using pastry brush or back of a spoon. Combine sugar and cinnamon in a small bowl, and sprinkle evenly over dough. Staring with the longest side, roll dough into a log.

(continued)

Combine corn syrup, brown sugar and remaining ¼ cup butter in small saucepan. Cook over low heat, stirring frequently, until butter is melted and mixture is smooth. Pour evenly into bottom of well-greased 10" x 15" baking pan. Sprinkle pecans evenly over.

Slice the dough into 1 ½" to 2" pieces and place close together (flat side down) over pecans in pan.

Cover with plastic wrap and let rise again until doubled in size (about ½ an hour). Bake for 25 minutes, or until cake tester inserted halfway comes out clean.

Remove from oven, let rest for 2 to 3 minutes, then unmold onto serving tray. Let cool slightly, and serve warm or cold. (Makes about 20 rolls.)

CAKES & ICINGS:

MIX AND MATCH FLAVORS

	Boiled White Icing, p. 99	Broiled Coconut Frosting, p. 27	Brown Sugar Frosting, p. 105
Autumn Spice Cake, p. 108		✓	✓
Banana Nut Cake, p. 33	✓	✓	✓
Black Walnut Cake, p. 101			✓
Blueberry Cream Cheese Cake, p. 77			
Coconut Cake, p. 87	✓		
Cool and Fruity Lemon Cake, p. 24	✓	✓	
Date Spice Cake, p. 85			✓
Devils Food Cream Cheese Cake, p. 116	✓		
Honey Citrus Cake, p. 36	✓	✓	
Lemon Cream Cheese Swirl Cake, p. 30	✓		
Never-ending Chocolate Bundt Cake, p. 78	✓		
Oatmeal Spice Cake, p. 104			✓
Orange Banana Bundt Cake, p. 95	✓		
White Chocolate Bundt Cake, p. 80	✓		

The possible combinations of cakes and icings are almost endless. So, we've listed only a few of the many flavor combinations that work well together in this handy table. When you're in the mood for a little variety, try some of the suggested pairings. Don't be limited by what you see here, however. Use your own creativity and likes to match other cake and icing combinations to suit your tastes!

Butter Pecan Frosting p. 111	Chocolate Fudge Icing, p. 103	Cream Cheese Icing, p. 107	Maple Frosting p. 101	Whipped Topping p. 25	White Frosting p. 115
●		●	●		
●		●		●	●
			●		
		●		●	●
	●	●		●	●
		●		●	●
			●		
	●	●			●
		●		●	●
		●		●	●
	●	●			●
●			●		
	●	●		●	●
	●				●

My Notes

Just Snap Your Fingers

You'll be amazed at the wide range of cookie styles and flavors you can create by using a cookie mix or cake mix as a base. For instance, the plain flavor of a sugar cookie mix provides a starting point for creating all kinds of great-tasting and great-looking cookies with the addition of a few simple ingredients. A cake mix can be used to create drop cookies or rolled cookies in less time than it would normally take to make a batch from scratch.

Thumbprint cookies, round cookies with a jam-filled center, look pretty and taste great. By adding a few ingredients to a humble sugar cookie dough, you can turn out a variety of tasty cookies in little time at all.

Follow the basic thumbprint cookie recipe, using the ingredients specified in the variations that follow to create a range of colorful, attractive, delicious cookies.

To speed your cookie-making, prepare the cookie dough the day before (it takes about 5 minutes), then tightly cover and refrigerate it until you're ready to use it. You'll be far ahead of the game when you're ready to bake.

BASIC THUMBPRINT
COOKIE RECIPE

1 (17.5 ounce) sugar cookie mix
½ cup (1 stick) butter or margarine, melted
1 egg
⅓ cup flour
1 egg white (if specified in recipe variation)
1 ¼ to 1 ½ cups chopped nuts or coconut, or
    ¼ cup sugar (see specific recipe instructions)
⅓ to ½ cup jam

Preheat oven to 375°. In medium bowl, combine cookie mix, melted butter and egg. Gradually stir in flour until dough is well blended.

Take dough by teaspoonfuls, and roll into balls between palms of your hands. Then depending upon recipe instructions, either roll each ball in sugar, or dip in egg white and then roll in ground nuts.

Place 2" to 3" apart on ungreased cookie sheet, and using blunt handle of spoon or your thumb, make slight depression in top of each cookie (make it about half the depth of the cookie). Fill with ½ teaspoonful of jam.

Bake for 10 to 13 minutes, or until edges are lightly browned. Remove from oven and cool on cookie sheet for a minute, then transfer to cooling rack.

VARIATIONS

Cherry Almond
Add 1 teaspoon almond extract to cookie mix, along with butter and egg. Dip balls in egg white, then roll in finely chopped or ground almonds. Fill with cherry jam. (Makes about 2 ½ to 3 dozen.)

Chocolate Raspberry
Add ¼ teaspoon almond extract and 3 tablespoons unsweetened cocoa powder to the dough. Roll balls in sugar. Fill with raspberry jam. (Makes 2 ½ to 3 dozen.)

Cinnamon Orange
Add 1 teaspoon cinnamon to cookie mix. Dip balls in egg white, then roll in finely chopped or ground walnuts. Fill with orange marmalade. (Makes 3 to 3 ½ dozen.)

Island Pineapple
Add 1 teaspoon lemon flavoring to cookie mix. Dip balls in egg white, then roll in coconut. Fill with pineapple jam. (Makes 3 to 3 ½ dozen.)

Peanut Butter and Jelly
Add ½ cup creamy peanut butter to dough before adding flour. Increase flour to ½ cup. Roll in sugar. Fill with grape jam. (Makes 3 ½ to 4 dozen.)

Chocolate Cherry

Add 1 tablespoon cocoa powder to cookie mix. Stir in ½ cup mini semi-sweet chocolate chips. Roll in sugar. Fill with cherry jam. (Makes about 3 dozen.)

Spicy Mincemeat

Add 1 teaspoon cinnamon to cookie mix. Dip balls in egg white, then roll in finely chopped or ground walnuts. Fill with mincemeat. (Makes about 3 dozen.)

Holiday Fruitcake

Add 1 teaspoon allspice and ½ cup fruitcake mix (or combination of finely chopped glaceed fruit). Roll in sugar. Fill with cherry jam.

Apricot Anisette

Add 1 teaspoon anise extract and 1 teaspoon lemon zest. Dip balls in egg white, then roll in chopped almonds. Fill with apricot jam.

OATMEAL ORANGE DATE COOKIES

1 (17.5 ounce) oatmeal cookie mix
½ cup flour
⅓ cup butter or margarine, melted
1 egg
¾ cup marmalade
½ cup chopped dates
¾ cup shredded coconut
¾ cup chopped walnuts

Preheat oven to 375°. In medium bowl, combine cookie mix and flour. Add butter, egg, and marmalade and mix well to blend.

Stir in dates, coconut, and walnuts.

Drop by heaping teaspoonful onto greased cookie sheet. Bake for 10 to 12 minutes. Let cookies cool on baking sheet for 1 minute before transferring to cooling rack. (Makes 3 dozen.)

MALTED MILK BALL CHOCOLATE CHIP COOKIES

1 (17.5 ounce) chocolate chip cookie mix
½ cup (1 stick) butter or margarine, softened
1 egg
1 cup crushed malted milk balls
½ cup chopped pecans

Preheat oven to 350°. In medium bowl, combine cookie mix, butter, and egg. Mix well.

Stir in malted milk balls and pecans and blend well.

Drop by heaping teaspoonful onto greased cookie sheet, and bake for 12-15 minutes.

Remove from oven, and let cookies cool on cookie sheet for 1 minute. Transfer to cooling rack. (Makes about 2 ½ to 3 dozen.)

CREAM CHEESE APRICOT COOKIES

4 ounces cream cheese, softened
¼ cup (½ stick) butter or margarine, softened
1 egg
1 (17.5 ounce) sugar cookie mix
½ cup dried chopped apricots

 Preheat oven to 375°. In medium bowl, cream cheese and butter until well blended. Add egg and beat until smooth. Stir in cookie mix (mixture will be thick). Stir in apricots.

Drop by rounded teaspoonful onto ungreased cookie sheet. Bake for 12 to 14 minutes, or until edges are lightly browned.

Remove from oven and let cookies cool on cookie sheet for 1 minute before transferring to cooling rack.

Because I really do not like the tedious job of chopping apricots, I like to use the Sunsweet brand "Fruitlings." These dried fruits are already cut in a size perfect for baking.

OATMEAL RAISIN COOKIES

1 (18.25 ounce) spice cake mix
1 cup quick-cooking oats
1 cup (2 sticks) butter or margarine, melted
1 egg
½ cup milk
1 teaspoon vanilla
¾ cup chopped walnuts
1 cup raisins

 Preheat oven to 350°. In large bowl, beat cake mix, oats, butter, egg, milk and vanilla until thoroughly blended. Mix in walnuts and raisins.

 Drop by rounded teaspoonful onto ungreased cookie sheet, and bake for 9 to 11 minutes. Let cool on cookie sheet for 1 minute, and then transfer to cooling rack.

ORANGE DATE WALNUT COOKIES

These delightful cookies are crispy and light, with just a hint of cinnamon.

1 (17.5 ounce) sugar cookie mix
½ cup (1 stick) butter or margarine, melted
1 egg
1 teaspoon orange extract
½ teaspoon cinnamon
½ cup chopped dates
½ cup coarsely chopped walnuts

Preheat oven to 375°. Combine cookie mix, butter, egg, orange extract and cinnamon in medium bowl. Blend well.

Stir in dates and walnuts.

Drop by heaping teaspoonful onto ungreased cookie sheet. Bake for 9 to 10 minutes, or until lightly browned around edges.

Remove cookies from oven and let cool on cookie sheet for 1 minute before transferring to cooling rack.

MOLASSES SPICE COOKIES

1 (17.5 ounce) sugar cookie mix
½ teaspoon ground ginger
¼ teaspoon nutmeg
1 teaspoon cinnamon
Pinch ground cloves
2 eggs
½ cup (1 stick) butter or margarine, melted
¼ cup molasses
½ cup raisins (optional)

Preheat oven to 375°. In large bowl, combine cookie mix, ginger, nutmeg, cinnamon and cloves. Stir thoroughly to mix.

Add eggs, butter and molasses. Mix well. If desired, stir in raisins.

Drop by rounded teaspoonful onto well greased cookie sheet. Bake for 7 to 9 minutes, or until lightly browned around edges.

Let cookies cool on cookie sheet for 1 minute, then transfer to cooling rack. (Makes 2 to 3 dozen.)

TRAIL MIX COOKIES

1 (17.5 ounce) oatmeal cookie mix
3 tablespoons water
⅓ cup vegetable oil
1 egg
1 cup (6 ounces) trail mix (containing chocolate candy,
   raisins, cashews and almonds)

Preheat oven to 350°. In medium bowl, combine cookie mix, water, oil and egg. Mix well.

Stir in trail mix.

Drop by heaping teaspoonful onto ungreased cookie sheet.

Bake for 10 to 12 minutes, or until edges are lightly browned. Remove from oven and let cool on cookie sheet for 1 minute. Transfer to cooling rack. (Makes 2 to 2 ½ dozen.)

COCONUT MACAROONS

1 (18.25 ounce) French vanilla cake mix (or white cake mix) with pudding
½ cup (1 stick) butter or margarine
3 eggs
1 teaspoon vanilla
½ cup sugar
3 cups shredded coconut

Preheat oven to 350°. In large bowl, combine cake mix, butter, eggs, vanilla and sugar. Beat on medium speed until well blended.

Stir in coconut. Drop by rounded teaspoonful onto ungreased cookie sheet.

Bake for 10 to 12 minutes. Let cookies cool on cookie sheet for 1 minute, then transfer to wire cooling rack. (Makes approximately 3 dozen.)

WHITE CHOCOLATE MACADAMIA NUT COOKIES

1 (18.25 ounce) white cake mix with pudding
½ cup (1 stick) butter or margarine
2 eggs
1 cup white chocolate baking chips
¾ cup coarsely chopped macadamia nuts, toasted*

Preheat oven to 350°. In medium bowl, combine cake mix, butter and eggs. Beat on medium speed until well blended. Stir in white chocolate chips and nuts.

Drop by rounded teaspoonful onto ungreased cookie sheet. Bake for 10 to 12 minutes. Cool cookies for 1 minute on baking sheet, and then transfer to wire rack. (Makes about 3 dozen.)

*See "Toasting Pecans" on page 111.

ORANGE PECAN COOKIES

1 (17.5 ounce) sugar cookie mix
½ cup (1 stick) butter or margarine, melted
1 egg
1 teaspoon orange extract
½ cup chopped pecans

Preheat oven to 350°. In medium bowl, combine cookie mix, butter, egg, orange extract and pecans. Mix well.

Drop by heaping teaspoonsful onto ungreased cookie sheet. Bake for 12 to 13 minutes, or until lightly browned around edges.

Remove from oven and let cool on cookie sheet for one minute. Transfer cookies to cooling rack. (Makes 2 to 2 ½ dozen.)

CHOCOLATEY CHOCOLATE CHIP OATMEAL COOKIES

½ cup (1 stick) butter or margarine, softened
2 eggs
1 (18.25 ounce) German chocolate cake mix
¾ cup old-fashioned oats
¾ cup semi-sweet chocolate chips
½ cup coarsely chopped pecans

Preheat oven to 375°. In large bowl, blend butter with eggs. Stir in cake mix and oats. Blend well.

Stir in chocolate chips and pecans.

Drop by heaping teaspoonful onto greased cookie sheet. Bake for 10 to 12 minutes (until edges are slightly browned). Remove from oven and let cool on cookie sheet for 1 minute. Remove cookies to cooling rack.

MINT CHOCOLATE COOKIES

1 (18.25 ounce) Swiss chocolate cake mix
1 egg
4 ounces frozen whipped topping, thawed
¼ teaspoon peppermint extract
Powdered sugar

Preheat oven to 350°. In large bowl, combine cake
mix, egg, whipped topping and peppermint extract.

Blend on low speed until thoroughly mixed.

Take heaping teaspoonfuls of dough and roll into
balls, then roll in powdered sugar. Place 3" apart on
greased cookie sheet and bake for 10 to 12 minutes.

NO-BAKE BUTTERSCOTCH COOKIES

More like a candy than a cookie,
these little butterscotch treats are delightful.

2 cups sugar
¾ cup (1 ½ sticks) butter or margarine
⅔ cup evaporated milk
1 (3.4 ounce) package butterscotch flavor instant
  pudding mix
3 ½ cups old-fashioned oats
¾ cup butterscotch baking chips
½ cup chopped pecans

In medium saucepan, bring sugar, butter and evaporated milk to a boil, stirring constantly. Boil for 1 minute, then remove from heat.

Stir in pudding mix, then oats and mix well. Cool for 10 minutes, then stir in butterscotch chips and pecans. (Note: butterscotch chips will melt, so stir until mixture is smooth.)

Drop by heaping teaspoonful onto waxed paper and let harden. (Makes 3 to 4 dozen.)

Variation for chocolate lovers:
Substitute chocolate fudge flavor pudding mix for the butterscotch, and omit the butterscotch chips.

SPICY OATMEAL COOKIES

¼ cup packed brown sugar
¼ cup sugar
¾ cup flour
½ teaspoon baking soda
Pinch salt
5 (1.51 ounce) raisins and spice flavor instant oatmeal
    packets
½ cup (1 stick) butter or margarine, softened
1 egg
½ teaspoon vanilla

Preheat oven to 350°. In large bowl, combine sugars, flour, baking soda, salt and oatmeal.

In small bowl, combine butter, egg and vanilla and mix well. Add to dry ingredients and blend thoroughly.

Drop by heaping teaspoonful onto ungreased cookie sheet, and bake for 12-14 minutes until nicely browned. Cool on cookie sheet for 1 minute, and then transfer to wire rack. (Makes 1 ½ to 2 dozen.)

DOUBLE CHOCOLATE CHIP COOKIES

1 (18.25 ounce) chocolate cake mix with pudding
½ cup (1 stick) butter or margarine
1 teaspoon vanilla
2 eggs
1 cup semi-sweet chocolate chips
¾ cup chopped pecans

Preheat oven to 350°. In medium bowl, combine cake mix, butter, vanilla and eggs. Beat on medium speed until well blended.

Stir in chocolate chips and pecans.

Drop by rounded teaspoonful onto ungreased cookie sheet and bake for 10 to 12 minutes. Cool for 1 minute on cookie sheet, and then remove to wire rack. (Makes about 3 dozen.)

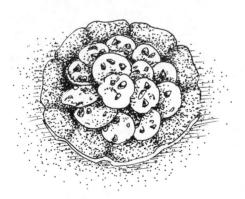

BANANA BUTTER PECAN COOKIES

1 (17.5 ounce) oatmeal cookie mix
1 egg
5 tablespoons butter, melted
¾ cup mashed bananas
¾ cup chopped pecans

Preheat oven to 375°. In large bowl, combine cookie mix with egg, butter and bananas. Mix well.

Stir in chopped pecans until well blended.

Drop by heaping teaspoonful onto lightly greased cookie sheet, and bake for 9 to 10 minutes, or until lightly browned around edges.

Let cool on cookie sheet for 1 minute, then transfer to cooling rack. (Makes 2 ½ to 3 dozen.)

MOCHA CINNAMON SNAPS

For an extra special finishing touch, I usually press a whole pecan lightly into the surface of each dough ball before baking. With the chocolate drizzled over, these cookies look like little gourmet treats—no one would ever guess how fast and easy they were to make.

1 (17.5 ounce) sugar cookie mix
2 tablespoons unsweetened cocoa
2 teaspoons cinnamon
1 teaspoon instant coffee granules
½ cup (1 stick) butter or margarine, melted
1 egg

Preheat oven to 375°. In medium bowl, combine cookie mix, cocoa, cinnamon and coffee. Mix well.

Add butter and egg and mix dough thoroughly.

Drop by rounded teaspoonfuls onto ungreased cookie sheet. Bake for 10 minutes. Let cool on cookie sheet for 1 minute, then transfer to cooling rack.

When cool, drizzle Chocolate Glaze over (use a zig-zag motion to make lines of chocolate across cookie surface). Makes 3 dozen.

(continued)

Chocolate Glaze
½ cup milk chocolate or semi-sweet chocolate
  chips
1 teaspoon shortening

In small saucepan, combine chocolate and shortening. Cook over low heat, stirring constantly, until chocolate is melted. (Or, place chocolate and shortening in small microwavable bowl, and cook on low power for 2 to 4 minutes, stopping after each minute to stir.)

Make drizzling easier by placing melted chocolate mixture in a plastic bag (like a sandwich bag), twist bag above the chocolate, and snip a tiny piece of the corner. Squeeze gently to dispense glaze.

If you're in a hurry, dropping these cookies by teaspoonful does the trick—but to make a really pretty, perfectly symmetrical cookie, take the teaspoonful of dough and roll it into a ball before placing it on the cookie sheet. As the cookie bakes, it will become round and smooth.

ICED LEMON POPPY SEED COOKIES

These cookies are "cakey" and very light. They mound slightly when they bake.

1 (18.25 ounce) lemon cake mix
1 (8 ounce) container sour cream
1 egg
2 tablespoons butter or margarine, softened
3 tablespoons poppy seed filling
¼ teaspoon almond extract

Preheat oven to 350°. In large bowl, combine cake mix, sour cream, egg, butter, poppy seeds and almond extract. Mix well by hand or with electric mixer on low speed until well blended.

Drop by rounded teaspoonsful 2" apart onto greased cookie sheets.

Bake for 11 to 13 minutes, or until golden brown. Cool for 1 minute on cookie sheets, then transfer to cooling rack. (Makes 2 ½ to 3 dozen.)

When cool, drizzle Powdered Sugar Glaze over.

(continued)

Powdered Sugar Glaze
1 cup powdered sugar
1 tablespoon, plus 1 teaspoon milk
¼ teaspoon almond extract

 In small bowl, stir milk and almond extract into powdered sugar until mixture is smooth. Drizzle over cookies in a zig-zag fashion.

To drizzle glaze over cookies, I put it in a plastic bag (like a sandwich bag) and snip a tiny piece off the corner. I then twist the top of the bag above the icing and squeeze lightly to dispense it.

BLACK FOREST CHERRY COOKIES

These cookies look and taste great even without the frosting.

1 (17.5 ounce) sugar cookie mix
½ cup (1 stick) butter or margarine, melted
1 egg
½ cup mini semi-sweet chocolate chips
½ cup quartered maraschino cherries

Preheat oven to 375°. In medium bowl, combine cookie mix, butter and egg. Mix well.

Stir in chocolate chips and maraschino cherries.

Drop by rounded teaspoonful onto an ungreased cookie sheet. Bake for 9 to 10 minutes, or until edges are lightly browned. Cool cookies on cookie sheets for 1 minute before transferring to cooling rack. When cool, frost with Chocolate Frosting, if desired.

(continued)

Chocolate Frosting
3 (1 ounce) squares semi-sweet chocolate
2 tablespoons butter
2 cups powdered sugar
2 tablespoons half-and-half (or milk)
1 to 2 tablespoons maraschino cherry syrup

Combine chocolate and butter in small saucepan. Cook over low heat, stirring constantly, until chocolate is melted. Remove from heat and let cool slightly.

In medium bowl, combine chocolate mixture with ½ cup powdered sugar; mix well.

Add half-and-half and cherry syrup (start with 1 tablespoon and add a little more syrup if needed), and beat until mixture is smooth.

Gradually add remaining powdered sugar, beating after each addition until mixture is smooth and reaches frosting consistency.

MAPLE ICED WALNUT COOKIES

1 (18.25 ounce) white cake mix
⅓ cup milk
4 tablespoons (½ stick) butter or margarine
1 egg
½ cup packed brown sugar
1 ½ cup coarsely chopped walnuts

Preheat oven to 350°. In large bowl, combine cake mix, milk, butter, egg and brown sugar. Beat on low speed until well blended, about 2 minutes.

Stir in walnuts, and drop by rounded teaspoonful onto lightly greased cookie sheet. Bake for 11-13 minutes, until lightly browned. Remove from oven and let cool for 1 minute, then transfer to cooling rack. When cool, frost with Maple Icing.

Maple Icing
1 ½ cups powdered sugar
3 tablespoons butter or margarine, softened
¼ cup maple syrup

In medium bowl, cream some of the powdered sugar (about ½ cup) with butter and maple syrup until smooth. Add remaining powdered sugar ½ cup at a time, beating after each addition, until frosting reaches spreading consistency.

CHOCOLATE PINWHEELS

1 (17.5 ounce) sugar cookie mix
⅓ cup flour
½ cup (1 stick) butter or margarine, melted
1 egg
1 (1 ounce) square semi-sweet baking chocolate, melted

- Preheat oven to 375°. In medium bowl, combine cookie mix, flour, butter and egg. Mix thoroughly.

- Divide dough in half. To one half, add the melted chocolate and mix until completely blended. (Refrigerate dough until chilled, if possible, to make it easier to work with.)

- On well floured surface, roll out white dough into a rectangle about ¼" thick. Then on another floured surface, roll out chocolate dough to same dimensions. Carefully lift chocolate dough and place over white dough. Roll from longest side jelly-roll fashion.

- Slice dough roll into pieces ¼" thick and place 3" apart on greased cookie sheet. Bake for about 10 minutes, or until edges are lightly browned. Remove from oven and place on cooling rack. (Makes 2 to 3 dozen.)

DATE NUT PINWHEEL COOKIES

1 cup finely chopped dates
½ cup sugar
½ cup water
½ cup chopped walnuts
1 (17.5 ounce) sugar cookie mix
¼ cup flour

In small sauce pan, combine dates, sugar and water. Bring to a simmer and cook for 3 minutes on medium heat until thickened. Remove from heat and let cool. Set aside.

Prepare cookie mix as directed on package, adding flour so that it will roll out more easily. Divide dough in half, and roll out one half into a rectangle ¼" thick.

Spread half the filling mixture evenly over the rolled out cookie dough. Sprinkle nuts evenly over mixture. Starting from long end, roll dough in jellyroll fashion. Wrap in plastic wrap and refrigerate until firm. Repeat with remaining dough and filling mixture.

Pinwheel Cookies

(Continued)

Preheat oven to 400°. Cut rolls into slices ¼" thick, and place 2 inches apart on lightly greased baking sheet.

Bake for 10 to 12 minutes, or until lightly browned. Remove from oven and place on cooling rack.

GINGER JAM SANDWICH COOKIES

These cookies make a really fast, tasty treat to take to a luncheon or other get together. They're really pretty just the way they are after you put them together, but look extra special with a little powdered sugar sifted on top.

1 (17.5 ounce) sugar cookie mix
2 teaspoons powdered ginger
½ teaspoon cinnamon
¼ teaspoon ground cloves
½ cup (1 stick) butter or margarine, melted
1 egg
½ cup strawberry jam

Preheat oven to 375°. In medium bowl, combine cookie mix with ginger, cinnamon and cloves. Stir well to blend. Add butter and egg, and mix thoroughly.

(continued)

Take small pieces of dough and roll into balls about ¾" to 1" in diameter.

Place 2" to 3" apart on ungreased cookie sheet, and bake for 9 to 10 minutes. Transfer cookies to cooling rack.

When completely cool, place ½ teaspoonful of jam in center of flat side of one cookie and top with flat side of another cookie, pressing lightly to distribute jam to edges. (Makes 2 ½ to 3 dozen.)

HOLIDAY CREME-FILLED SANDWICH COOKIES

It's always fun to have baked goods that reflect the holiday spirit. The cookies that follow are all created from one simple sandwich cookie recipe: a plain sugar cookie colored and sometimes flavored, combined with a complementary filling.

Simply follow the instructions for the basic dough and filling recipes below, modifying them as outlined in the variations that follow.

Basic Dough Recipe
1 (17.5 ounce) sugar cookie mix
½ cup (1 stick) butter or margarine, melted
1 egg

In medium bowl, blend sugar cookie mix with butter and egg. Mix well.

Preheat oven to 375°. Roll dough into balls 1" in diameter. (Be sure and make each ball the same size, so that your cookies will be even when you put them together. Also be sure that you make an even amount of cookies, so that you'll have complete sandwiches.)

(continued)

- Place 2" apart on ungreased cookie sheet. Bake for 8 to 10 minutes (try not to let edges get brown; if they do, reduce the baking time slightly).

- Let cookies cool on cookie sheet for 1 minute, then transfer onto cooling rack. When cool, place approximately 1 teaspoon filling in center back of one cookie. Place another cookie on top (flat side over filling), and using even pressure, press down in middle of top cookie to force filling outward to cookie edges.

Basic Creme Filling
6 tablespoons butter or margarine, softened
½ teaspoon flavoring (if specified)
1 ½ cups powdered sugar
1 to 1 ½ tablespoons half-and-half or milk

- In medium bowl, cream butter and half of powdered sugar.

- Add 1 tablespoon half-and-half and beat well.

- Add remaining powdered sugar and enough half-and-half to make filling easy to work with, but not too thin.

Halloween Orange and Chocolate Cookies

Make sugar cookie dough and add ½ teaspoon orange extract with butter and egg. Add 4 drops of red food coloring and 8 drops of yellow to make dough orange.

Add 3 tablespoons cocoa powder to filling.

Variation:

You can also make the reverse of the cookies above by making the cookies chocolate and the filling orange. Add 2 tablespoons cocoa powder to the sugar cookie mix, before adding the butter and egg.

To make orange colored filling, add 2 drops of red food coloring and 4 drops of yellow. If desired, add ¼ teaspoon orange extract to flavor the filling.

(I actually like to make a batch of each, and mix them on a serving tray.)

Peppermint Christmas Cookies

Make sugar cookie dough. Divide dough in half. Add 10 drops of red food coloring to one half of dough. Mix well so that dough is evenly colored. Add 10 drops of green to the other half, and mix well.

(continued)

Add ½ teaspoon peppermint extract to filling.

To make cookies, place one green and one red cookie together, with filling in the middle.

Valentine's Day Cheery-Cherry Cookies

Make sugar cookie dough. Add 10 drops of red food coloring to dough, but mix dough only enough to get a marbled effect, not to evenly color it.

Add ⅓ cup minced maraschino cherries and ½ teaspoon clear vanilla flavoring to filling.

Pretty Pastel Easter Cookies

Make sugar cookie dough. Divide into thirds. Color one third peach by adding 1 drop of red food coloring and 3 drops of yellow. Color another third purple by adding 3 drops of blue food coloring and 3 drops of red. Color the remaining third light green by adding 3 drops of green food coloring.

To filling add ½ teaspoon lemon extract.

CHOCOLATE TURTLE COOKIES

This cookie version of the classic candy looks and tastes as good as it sounds. The turtle shapes are so easy (and cute!). Because you start with a cake mix, you can have the first batch of cookies out of the oven in no time.

1 (18.25 ounce) German chocolate or devil's food cake
   mix with pudding
½ cup (1 stick) butter or margarine, softened
1 teaspoon vanilla
2 eggs
4 to 5 cups pecan halves

Preheat oven to 350°. In medium bowl, combine cake mix, butter, vanilla and eggs; beat on medium speed until well blended.

Drop by small rounded teaspoonful onto greased cookie sheet, leaving enough room to add pecans to edges without crowding cookies.

For each cookie, arrange five pecan halves in a star shape around dough—one for the head, and four for legs—letting pecans just butt up against the dough. As the cookies bake they will flatten and expand to partially cover the pecans.

Bake for 12 to 15 minutes. Remove from oven and cool for 2 minutes on cookie sheet before removing to cooling rack. Cool slightly, and top with Caramel Topping.

(continued)

Caramel Topping

1 (14 ounce) bag (about 44) individually-wrapped
  caramel candies, unwrapped
2 tablespoons half-and-half or milk
2 tablespoons butter or margarine

In top of double boiler over boiling water, combine
caramels, half-and-half, and butter. Cook, stirring
frequently, until caramels melt. Remove from heat,
but keep double boiler intact, so caramel remains
soft as you frost cookies. Place a small spoonful of
caramel in center of cookie, and smooth to edges of
cookie with butter knife or spatula.

Save some time by making the caramel topping while
the first batch of cookies bakes. It can remain warm
in the double boiler and be ready for the first batch
of cookies after they've cooled for a couple of
minutes.

Also, you'll want to be sure to pick the nicest,
plumpest pecans for these. (Note: I have tried
making these with a cake mix that didn't contain
pudding, and they didn't come out as nicely. They
were too thin.)

SPICY CINNAMON TWISTS

1 (17.5 ounce) sugar cookie mix
½ cup flour
½ cup (1 stick) butter or margarine, melted
1 egg
1 teaspoon maple flavoring
1 teaspoon allspice
1 teaspoon ginger
¼ cup sugar
1 teaspoon cinnamon

Preheat oven to 375°. In medium bowl, combine cookie mix, flour, butter, egg, maple flavoring, allspice and ginger. Mix well.

In small bowl, mix sugar and cinnamon. Pour into plate or shallow bowl. Set aside.

Roll heaping tablespoons of dough into ropes 6" long. Gently lift, fold in half (keeping loose ends even), and twist 3 times. Place on ungreased cookie sheet about 2" apart.

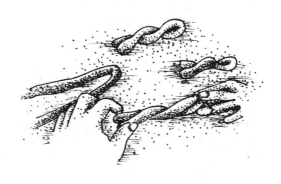

(continued)

Bake for 12 minutes, or until edges are lightly browned. Let cool on cookie sheet for 1 minute, and then remove to cooling rack. Let cool for several minutes, then press surface into sugar cinnamon mixture.

GINGERBREAD ROLLED COOKIES

These cookies are great! They're a fast way to make a delicious rolled cookie. When you're swamped at Christmastime with the hustle and bustle of the holiday season, you'll find these are a great way to enjoy making holiday cookies without spending a lot of time mixing the dough. There's less to clean up too!

¾ cup (1 ½ sticks) butter or margarine, softened
2 egg yolks
1 (18.25 ounce) spice cake mix
1 teaspoon ginger

Preheat oven to 375°. In large bowl, combine butter and egg yolks. Gradually blend in cake mix and ginger. Mix well.

Roll dough out to ⅛" thickness on lightly floured surface. Cut shapes with cookie cutter and place 2" apart on ungreased cookie sheets.

Bake for 7 to 9 minutes, or until edges are lightly browned. Remove from oven and cool cookies for 1 minute on cookie sheets before transferring to cooling rack.

Special Cookies

(continued)

In order to roll the dough more easily and prevent it from sticking to the rolling pin, I place a piece of waxed paper over the dough first, and roll over it. Then I peel it away and cut out the cookies.

Also, to keep the cookies from stretching out of shape when I pick them up, I slide a thin spatula (or turner) under them and lift them onto the cookie sheet.

ORANGE CHOCOLATE FILLED COOKIES

1 (18.25 ounce) butter recipe yellow cake mix
2 egg yolks
2 teaspoons orange extract
¾ cup (1 ½ sticks) butter or margarine, softened
½ cup mini semi-sweet chocolate chips
½ cup chopped walnuts

Preheat oven to 375°. In large bowl, combine cake mix, egg yolks, orange extract and butter. Blend until thoroughly mixed.

Prepare filling. Combine chocolate chips and walnuts in blender or food processor. Blend for about 30 seconds, or until mixture starts to hold together.

Divide the dough in half, and work with one half at a time. (Refrigerate unused dough until ready to use.) Roll dough out on well floured surface to ⅛" thickness. Cut 2 ½" diameter circles using biscuit cutter or round cookie cutter.

Place 1 teaspoon of filling mixture in center of one circle, gently spreading it out, but not extending it to the edge. Place another cut out circle on top, and using very thin spatula (or turner) to lift entire cookie, place it on cookie sheet. Crimp the edges gently with a fork to seal. Repeat, allowing 3" between cookies on baking sheet.

(continued)

Bake cookies for 10 to 12 minutes, or until lightly browned around edges. Remove from oven and let cookies cool on cookie sheet for 1 minute before transferring to cooling rack.

When cool, glaze with Semi-sweet Chocolate Glaze. (I use a small plastic bag, like a sandwich bag, and fill it with the chocolate mixture, twist it above the mixture and snip the corner and then squeeze gently to dispense the glaze.)

Semi-sweet Chocolate Glaze
½ cup semi-sweet chocolate chips
1 teaspoon shortening

Melt chocolate and shortening in small saucepan over low heat, stirring constantly.

CHOCOLATE-DIPPED MALTED MILK COOKIES

The taste of malted milk balls in a cookie? Unbelievable! These round, crisp cookies have the color of the inside of a malted milk ball, and with the chocolate coating on one side, taste like them too.

1 (17.5 ounce) sugar cookie mix
½ cup malted milk powder
1 egg
½ cup (1 stick) butter or margarine, melted
1 ½ cups milk chocolate chips
1 tablespoon shortening

Preheat oven to 375°. In medium bowl, combine cookie mix, malted milk powder, egg and butter. Mix well. Using your hands, roll heaping teaspoonfuls of dough into balls and place 3" apart on ungreased cookie sheet.

Bake for 9 to 11 minutes, just until edges are browned. Let cookies cool on baking pan for 1 minute before transferring to cooling rack.

In small saucepan over low heat, melt chocolate in shortening, stirring constantly. Remove from heat. Coat cooled cookie by tilting pan and dipping half of cookie into chocolate glaze. Gently shake off excess chocolate and place cookie on waxed paper. Leave cookies on waxed paper for about an hour to set chocolate. Store cookies in covered container in single layers with waxed paper between them.

Stir Up Some Dreamy Delights . . .

Bars 196

Cake, brownie, and cookie mixes can be used to create an amazing assortment of delicious bars—everything from cake-like bars to chewy, dense, brownie-like bars, to crunchy-topped, jam-filled bars. The following pages contain recipes covering a range of flavor combinations.

The great thing about using a mix for bar cookies is ease of use. Just like with the cakes, most of the recipes that follow use a few additional ingredients to create different desserts in a snap.

PINEAPPLE MACADAMIA NUT BARS

These cake-like bars are chock-full of macadamia nut flavor.

1 (18.25 ounce) white cake mix
¼ cup (½ stick) butter or margarine, melted
¼ cup packed brown sugar
1 (8 ounce) can crushed pineapple, well drained, juice
   reserved
¼ cup reserved pineapple juice
2 eggs
¾ cup chopped macadamia nuts, toasted

Preheat oven to 375°. In large bowl, combine cake
mix, butter, brown sugar, pineapple, pineapple juice
and eggs. Beat on low speed or by hand until well-
blended (about 1 minute).

Stir in macadamia nuts and spread batter into
greased and floured 9" x 13" baking pan. Bake for
20 minutes, or until golden brown. Remove from
oven and let cool slightly, then frost with Pineapple
Icing.

Pineapple Icing
2 tablespoons butter or margarine, softened
2 tablespoons reserved pineapple juice
Pinch of salt
2 cups powdered sugar

In small bowl, cream butter with pineapple juice, salt
and ½ cup powdered sugar. Add remaining powdered
sugar a little at a time, blending well after each
addition. Spread on warm bars.

LEMON GLAZED PECAN BARS

The pecan and lemon combination in these bars is a little unusual, but really very good. These bars are very similar to pecan pie with a sweet cookie crust. Because they hold together well, they're very portable and make a good dessert to take to a get together.

1 (17.5 ounce) package sugar cookie mix, prepared
   as directed on package
3 eggs
1 cup packed dark brown sugar
1 cup chopped pecans, toasted*
1 cup coconut
2 teaspoons vanilla
½ cup powdered sugar
¼ cup fresh lemon juice
Zest of one small lemon

Preheat oven to 350°. Press cookie dough evenly in bottom of lightly greased and floured 9" x 13" baking pan. Bake for 15 minutes, or until lightly browned around the edges. Remove from oven and let cool for about 10 minutes.

While crust is baking, in medium bowl combine eggs, brown sugar, pecans, coconut and vanilla. Mix well. Pour over the warm crust and bake for another 15 to 20 minutes, until slightly browned on top.

To make the glaze, in a small bowl combine powdered sugar, lemon juice and lemon zest. Mix well. Either brush or drizzle glaze over the bars while they are still warm from the oven. Let them cool, and cut into bars.

*See "Toasting Pecans" on page 111.

CHOCOLATE PECAN PIE SQUARES

This is a versatile little dessert—the bars are great by themselves, but even better with the Caramel Sauce and Chocolate Whipped Cream. For a really decadent taste treat, serve them warm with a scoop of vanilla ice cream on top and a little warm caramel sauce drizzled over.

1 (17.5 ounce) sugar cookie mix
4 eggs, divided
¾ cup (1 ½ sticks) butter or margarine, divided
½ teaspoon cinnamon
1 (1 ounce) square semi-sweet chocolate
1 ½ cups packed brown sugar
2 tablespoons bourbon
1 teaspoon vanilla
1 cup coarsely chopped pecans

Preheat oven to 350°. Melt ½ cup butter in small saucepan. In medium bowl, combine cookie mix, 1 egg, melted butter and cinnamon.

Spread batter in bottom of lightly greased and floured 9" x 13" baking pan. Bake for 15 minutes, until lightly browned around edges.

In small saucepan, combine remaining butter and chocolate. Cook over low heat, stirring frequently, until both are melted. Immediately remove from heat. Let cool slightly.

In medium bowl, combine remaining eggs, brown sugar, bourbon and vanilla. Add cooled chocolate mixture and blend well. Stir in pecans. Pour mixture over cookie crust, and bake for 15 to 20 minutes. (Check after 15 minutes; if pecans are browned, remove from oven. Do not over bake.)

(continued)

(You can use either a purchased jar of caramel sauce or make the recipe below. It's a cinch to make and will only take you about 5 minutes.)

Caramel Sauce
6 tablespoons butter or margarine
¾ cup packed brown sugar
½ cup whipping cream

Combine butter and brown sugar in medium saucepan. Cook over medium heat, stirring constantly, until sugar dissolves.

Gradually add cream, stirring well after each addition, until mixture comes to a boil. Boil for 1 to 2 minutes and remove from heat. (Makes a little over 1 cup.) Store tightly covered in the refrigerator, and use as needed.

Chocolate Whipped Cream
½ cup whipping cream
1 tablespoon powdered sugar
1 tablespoon cocoa

In small chilled bowl, combine whipping cream, powdered sugar and cocoa; beat on high speed until stiff peaks form, stopping to scrape bowl occasionally as you beat. (Makes ¾ cup.)

LEMON RASPBERRY CRUMB BARS

The raspberries are not only colorful but they also add a nice tart flavor that goes well with the sweet lemon topping.

1 (18.25 ounce) yellow or white cake mix (with or without pudding)
½ cup (1 stick) butter or margarine, softened
1 egg
1 (14 ounce) can sweetened condensed milk
½ cup fresh lemon juice
½ pint fresh raspberries (a little over a cup)

Preheat oven to 350°. In large bowl, combine cake mix, butter and egg. Blend on low speed until crumbly. (Do not over mix, or mixture will become sticky.)

Reserve 2 cups of crumb mixture, and place remainder in greased 9" x 13" baking pan. Using fingers or turner, press mixture evenly into bottom of pan. Bake for 15 minutes.

While crust is baking, prepare topping. In medium bowl, combine sweetened condensed milk with lemon juice. Stir until well-blended. (Mixture will thicken as you stir.)

Arrange raspberries evenly over surface of partially cooked crust. Pour lemon mixture over raspberries as evenly as possible. (Coverage will be thin in some places.) Sprinkle reserved crumb mixture on top.

Bake for 20 minutes more, or until lightly browned on top. Cool and cut into bars. Keep refrigerated.

CHERRY ALMOND BARS

*These bars are moist and bursting with cherry flavor. When I
made them for my husband's friends at work, they raved about
them. You can actually make these a couple of days ahead, because
they keep very well.*

1 (18.25 ounce) white cake mix
⅓ cup (5 ⅓ tablespoons) butter or margarine,
  softened
1 (12 ounce) can cherry filling (like the one from Solo
  brand)
1 cup ground almonds
1 cup powdered sugar
1 teaspoon almond extract
4 egg whites

Preheat oven to 350°. In large bowl, combine cake
mix and butter. Beat on low speed until blended
(mixture will be crumbly); reserve ½ cup for topping.
Press remaining mixture into bottom of greased 9" x
13" baking pan.

Spread cherry filling gently over mixture as evenly as
possible. (It will be thin in some places.)

In same bowl, combine almonds, powdered sugar,
almond extract and egg whites; beat at high speed
for 4 minutes. Pour evenly over cherry filling.

Sprinkle ½ cup of reserved crumbs over egg white
mixture.

Bake for 20 to 25 minutes, or until lightly browned.
Cool and cut into bars.

PECAN PIE BARS

These scrumptious bars have a cake-like texture and are loaded with pecan pie flavor. I didn't realize how popular these had become in my family until my father requested them instead of a traditional cake for his birthday!

Crust
1 (18.25 ounce) yellow cake mix
1 egg
¼ cup (½ stick) butter or margarine, softened
1 cup shredded coconut
½ cup finely chopped pecans

Filling
1 cup sugar
3 eggs
½ teaspoon salt
1 cup corn syrup
¼ cup (½ stick) butter or margarine, melted
1 teaspoon vanilla
2 cups chopped pecans

Preheat oven to 350°. In large bowl, combine cake mix, egg, butter, coconut and pecans. Beat on low speed until well blended. (Mixture will be crumbly.)

Bars

(continued)

Press mixture into bottom of greased and floured 9" x 13" baking pan. Bake for about 13 minutes (edges should be lightly browned, but not too dark), and remove from oven.

While crust is baking, prepare filling. In medium bowl, combine sugar, eggs, salt, corn syrup, butter and vanilla. Beat on medium high speed until well blended and fluffy. Stir in pecans.

Pour filling over hot crust and return to oven. Bake for 25 to 30 minutes—until edges are brown and center is set. Cool and cut into bars.

LEMON APRICOT BARS

Lemon lovers everywhere—beware! Once you get started on these delicious bars, you won't be able to stop. They have a crisp crust with a gooey lemon filling spiked with the tang of apricots.

1 (17.5 ounce) sugar cookie mix
½ cup (1 stick) butter or margarine, melted
⅓ cup finely chopped pecans
5 eggs, divided
½ cup shredded coconut
2 cups sugar
2 tablespoons lemon zest (grated lemon rind)
¼ cup fresh lemon juice
1 teaspoon baking powder
½ teaspoon salt
1 cup shredded coconut
½ cup chopped dried apricots

Preheat oven to 350°. In medium bowl, combine cookie mix, butter, pecans and 1 egg. Mix well. Stir in coconut. With hands (or spatula) press mixture evenly into bottom of greased and floured 9" x 13" baking pan. Bake for 20 minutes. Remove from oven.

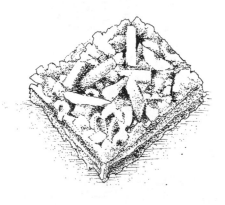

(continued)

🥄 In large bowl, combine sugar, lemon zest, lemon juice, baking powder, salt and remaining eggs. Beat with mixer on high speed for about 3 minutes (until light and fluffy). Stir in coconut and apricots. Pour over crust.

🥄 Bake for 25 minutes (or until no indentation remains when you press the top lightly). Remove from oven and cool completely. Cut into bars.

These bars were so yummy (and easy to make), I started thinking of other flavor combinations faster than I could make them! The two recipes that follow are variations that are just as good. These are so rich, they will satisfy any sweet tooth.

ORANGE WALNUT BARS

1 (17.5 ounce) oatmeal cookie mix
1 teaspoon cinnamon
⅓ cup vegetable oil
3 tablespoons water
5 eggs, divided
2 cups sugar
2 tablespoons orange zest (grated orange rind)
¼ cup orange juice
1 teaspoon baking powder
½ teaspoon salt
½ cup chopped walnuts
1 cup shredded coconut

Preheat oven to 350°. In medium bowl, combine cookie mix, cinnamon, oil, water and 1 egg. Mix well. With hands (or spatula) press mixture evenly into bottom of greased and floured 9" x 13" baking pan. Bake for 20 minutes. Remove from oven.

In large bowl, combine sugar, orange zest, orange juice, baking powder, salt and remaining eggs. Beat with mixer on high speed for about 3 minutes (until light and fluffy).

Stir in walnuts and coconut. Pour over crust.

Bake for 25 minutes. Remove from oven and cool completely. Cut into bars.

PINEAPPLE CHERRY BARS

1 (17.5 ounce) sugar cookie mix
½ cup (1 stick) butter or margarine, melted
5 eggs, divided
⅓ cup chopped almonds
2 cups sugar
¼ cup reserved pineapple juice
½ teaspoon almond extract
1 teaspoon baking powder
½ teaspoon salt
1 (8 ounce) can crushed pineapple, very well drained,
   juice reserved
1 cup coconut
½ cup maraschino cherries, well drained and
   quartered

Preheat oven to 350°. In medium bowl, combine
cookie mix, butter, 1 egg and almonds. Mix well.
With hands (or spatula) press mixture evenly into
bottom of greased and floured 9" x 13" baking pan.
Bake for 20 minutes. Remove from oven.

In large bowl, combine sugar, pineapple juice,
almond extract, baking powder, salt and remaining
eggs. Beat with mixer on high speed for about 3
minutes (until light and fluffy). Stir in pineapple,
coconut and cherries. Pour over crust.

Bake for 25 minutes. Remove from oven and cool
completely. Cut into bars.

PUMPKIN BARS

With their spicy flavor, these bars are a perfect snack for the Thanksgiving holidays.

½ cup (1 stick) butter or margarine, melted
1 cup packed light brown sugar
1 cup canned pumpkin
1 ½ cups flour
½ teaspoon baking soda
2 (1 5⁄8 ounce) cinnamon and spice flavor instant oatmeal packets
½ cup chopped pecans

Preheat oven to 350°. In medium bowl, combine butter, sugar and pumpkin; mix well.

In separate bowl, combine flour, baking soda, oatmeal and pecans; stir to blend. Add to pumpkin mixture, and mix thoroughly.

Spread evenly in greased 9" x 13" baking pan, and bake for 16 to 18 minutes. Immediately upon removing from oven pour glaze over bars. Let cool, and cut.

Glaze
1 cup powdered sugar
3 tablespoons orange juice

In small bowl, blend powdered sugar and orange juice.

BROWNIE BOTTOM CHEESECAKE WITH CHOCOLATE FROSTING

1 (18.25 ounce) devil's food cake mix (with or without pudding)
½ cup butter or margarine
3 eggs, divided
2 (8 ounce) packages cream cheese, softened
¾ cup sugar

Preheat oven to 325°. In large bowl, combine cake mix, butter and 1 egg; blend well. Press mixture into bottom of greased 9" x 13" baking pan.

In medium bowl, combine remaining eggs, cream cheese and sugar. Beat until mixture is smooth and well blended.

Pour mixture over cake mix, and bake for 40 to 45 minutes (until edges are very lightly browned). Let cool and ice with Chocolate Frosting.

Chocolate Frosting
1 cup semi-sweet chocolate chips
1 (8 ounce) container sour cream

In small saucepan, combine chocolate chips and sour cream. Cook over low to medium heat, stirring constantly, until chocolate melts and mixture is smooth. Remove from heat and let cool until just warm to the touch.

BUTTERSCOTCH BARS

1 (18.25 ounce) white cake mix
1 (3.4 oz) instant butterscotch pudding mix
1 cup milk
1 egg
1 cup chopped pecans
¾ cup butterscotch baking chips

 Preheat oven to 350°. In large bowl, combine cake mix, pudding mix, milk and egg. Beat on low speed until well blended (about 1 minute).

Stir in pecans and spread batter in greased and floured 9" x 13" baking pan.

Sprinkle butterscotch chips evenly over surface, and press lightly into batter. Bake for 30 to 35 minutes, until cake tester comes out clean.

CHERRY CHOCOLATE BARS

1 (18.25 ounce) devil's food cake mix
1 (20 ounce) can cherry pie filling
2 eggs
1 cup semi-sweet or milk chocolate chips

Preheat oven to 350°. In large bowl, combine all ingredients, blending well.

Pour batter into greased and floured 9" x 13" baking pan.

Bake for 25 to 30 minutes, or until cake tester comes out clean. Cool and frost with Chocolate Cream Cheese Frosting.

Chocolate Cream Cheese Frosting
3 (1 ounce) squares semi-sweet chocolate, melted
1 (3 ounce) package cream cheese, softened
½ teaspoon vanilla
1 ¼ cups powdered sugar

In medium bowl, beat chocolate with cream cheese and vanilla. Gradually beat in powdered sugar until frosting is smooth and well blended.

CHOCOLATE TOPPED TOFFEE BARS

1 (18.25 ounce) white cake mix
¼ cup (½ stick) butter or margarine, melted
¼ cup packed brown sugar
¼ cup milk
2 eggs
1 ½ cups toffee chips (or crushed Heath or Skor candy bars)
¾ cup chopped pecans

Preheat oven to 375°. In large bowl, combine cake mix, butter, brown sugar, milk and eggs. Beat on low speed to blend, about 2 minutes. Stir in toffee chips; then stir in pecans.

Spread batter in greased and floured 9" x 13" baking dish. Bake for 20 to 25 minutes, or until lightly browned.

When cool, drizzle with chocolate glaze.

(continued)

Chocolate Glaze
½ cup milk chocolate chips
2 teaspoons butter or shortening

Melt chocolate and shortening together in small
saucepan or in microwave at half-power (stirring
every 30 seconds until chocolate is melted and
mixture is smooth).

Variation
For a really chewy, moist bar, try adding the following
topping before baking. You'll need to add an additional
5 minutes to the baking time, but they turn out so
rich!

3 tablespoons butter or margarine, melted
1 cup packed brown sugar
1 cup shredded coconut

Combine butter with brown sugar and mix well. Stir
in coconut until it is thoroughly coated. Sprinkle
over batter just before baking. When cool, drizzle
with chocolate glaze.

CHOCOLATE DREAM BARS

1 (18.25 ounce) German chocolate cake mix
3 cups quick-cooking oats
1 cup (2 sticks) butter or margarine, melted
1 (14 ounce) can sweetened condensed milk
1 cup semi-sweet chocolate chips
1 cup shredded coconut
¾ cup chopped pecans

Preheat oven to 375°. In large bowl, combine cake mix and oats. Mix well. Add butter and beat mixture on low speed until it clumps together and all dry mix is moistened.

Press half of this mixture in a greased 9" x 13" baking pan. Pour condensed milk evenly over batter.

Sprinkle chocolate chips, coconut and pecans evenly over milk.

Crumble remaining mixture over, and bake for 20 minutes. Let cool well before cutting into bars.

HONEY-NUT OATMEAL JAM BARS

½ cup butter or margarine, softened
½ cup packed brown sugar
1 ¾ cups flour
Pinch salt
½ teaspoon baking soda
4 (1.51 ounce) honey nut flavor instant oatmeal
    packets
¾ cup strawberry jam

 Preheat oven to 400°. In large bowl, cream butter
and brown sugar. Add flour, salt, baking soda and
oatmeal; mix well. (Mixture will be crumbly.)

Press half of mixture firmly into bottom of a greased
8 x 8 baking pan. Spread jam over mixture. Top with
remaining crumbled mixture. Bake for 25 to 30
minutes, or until lightly browned. Cool slightly, and
cut into bars.

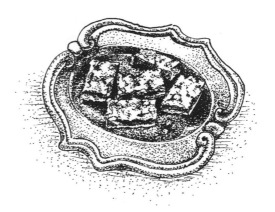

NO-BAKE CHOCOLATE OATMEAL BARS

These easy to make bars are hard to resist and disappear as fast as you make them.

2 cups sugar
½ cup sweetened condensed milk
1 (1 ounce) square unsweetened baking chocolate
½ cup (1 stick) butter or margarine
1 teaspoon vanilla
½ cup creamy peanut butter
Pinch of salt
½ cup chopped pecans
5 (1.51 oz) packets maple and brown sugar flavor instant oatmeal

In heavy saucepan, bring sugar, milk, chocolate and butter to a boil, then immediately remove from heat.

Add vanilla, peanut butter, salt, pecans and oatmeal. Stir well, and quickly press into greased 9" x 13" baking dish.

Cool slightly, and cut into bars.

APRICOT OATMEAL BARS

These bars are an example of how just a few ingredients (four to be exact) added to a cake mix can produce a tasty treat.

1 (18.25 ounce) yellow cake mix
3 cups old-fashioned oats
¾ cup chopped pecans
1 cup (2 sticks) butter or margarine, melted
1 ½ cups apricot jam

Preheat oven to 375°. In large bowl, combine cake mix, oats, pecans and butter. Mix well until entire mixture is crumbly.

Press half of this mixture evenly into bottom of a greased 9" x 13" baking pan. Spread apricot jam evenly over surface, and sprinkle remaining half of mixture evenly over jam.

Bake for 20 minutes, or until well-browned on top.

STRAWBERRY CREAM CHEESE BARS

If you like cheesecake, or pastries with cheese filling, you'll really like these bars. With the consistency of a brownie when baked, these bars come out of the oven topped with a thin layer of cheese similar to what you'd find in a cheese danish.

1 (18.25 ounce) strawberry cake mix (with or without pudding)
½ cup (1 stick) butter or margarine
3 eggs, divided
1 (8 ounce) package cream cheese, softened
2 cups powdered sugar

Preheat oven to 325°. In large bowl, combine cake mix, butter and 1 egg; blend well.

Press mixture into bottom of a greased 9" x 13" baking pan.

In medium bowl, beat cream cheese, 2 eggs and sugar until mixture is smooth and well blended.

Pour mixture over cake mix batter, and bake for 30 to 35 minutes (until lightly browned on top).

LEMON BUTTERMILK BARS

These bars are one of my all time favorites for their delicious flavor! Their delicate lemon taste, very moist texture, and crispy crust makes them taste a lot like buttermilk pie.

1 (18.25 ounce) lemon cake mix (with pudding), divided
4 eggs, divided
2 tablespoons vegetable oil
1 cup buttermilk
½ cup butter or margarine, melted
¾ cup sugar
1 teaspoon vanilla

Preheat oven to 350°. Reserve 1 cup dry cake mix and set aside.

In large bowl, combine remaining cake mix, 1 egg and oil; blend well. Press batter into bottom of greased 9" x 13" baking pan.

In medium bowl, beat remaining eggs, buttermilk, butter, sugar and vanilla until well blended. Slowly add reserved cake mix, and beat on medium speed until mixture is smooth (about 2 minutes).

Pour over batter in cake pan, and bake for 35 to 40 minutes, until lightly browned on top. Cool and cut into bars.

CHERRY CHEESE SQUARES

1 (18.25 ounce) white cake mix, with pudding in the
   mix
½ cup (1 stick) butter or margarine, melted
½ cup chopped almonds
1 ½ cups cherry preserves, divided (a 16 ounce sized
   jar is just shy of 1 ½ cups and will work fine)
1 (8 ounce) package cream cheese, softened
¼ cup sugar
2 tablespoons flour
1 egg
1 teaspoon almond extract
½ cup shredded coconut

Preheat oven to 350°. In large bowl, combine cake
mix and butter. Beat on low speed until mixture is
crumbly. Stir in almonds. Reserve 1 cup of mixture.

Press remaining mixture into bottom of greased
9" x 13" baking pan. Spread 1 cup of cherry
preserves over mixture to within ½" of edges of pan.

In medium bowl, beat cream cheese until smooth,
and add remaining preserves, sugar, flour, egg and
almond extract. Continue to beat, scraping bowl as
necessary, until mixture is smooth. Gently spread
on top of preserves to edge of pan.

(continued)

Combine coconut with reserved crumb mixture and sprinkle over cream cheese.

Bake for 25 to 30 minutes, or until lightly browned on top. Cool completely and cut into squares.

Variation

If you like the taste of citrus, you can make this same recipe with apricot preserves and a lemon cake mix. Just substitute apricot preserves for the cherry preserves, and a lemon cake mix for the white. You can also use clear vanilla flavoring instead of the almond if you want.

LEMON CHEESECAKE BARS WITH WHITE CHOCOLATE FROSTING

1 (18.25 ounce) lemon cake mix (with pudding)
½ cup (1 stick) butter or margarine, softened
3 eggs, divided
2 (8 ounce) packages cream cheese, softened
1 teaspoon vanilla
1 teaspoon lemon extract
2 cups powdered sugar

Preheat oven to 325°. In large bowl, combine cake mix, butter, and 1 egg. Beat on low speed until well blended. Spread batter into bottom of greased 9" x 13" baking pan.

In medium bowl, combine 2 eggs, cream cheese, vanilla, lemon extract and sugar. Beat on low speed to blend, and then beat on medium speed until mixture is smooth (from 1 to 2 minutes).

Pour over cake batter; bake for 40 to 45 minutes. Let cool, and frost with White Chocolate Frosting.

White Chocolate Frosting
1 cup white chocolate baking chips
1 (8 ounce) container sour cream

In small saucepan, heat white chocolate and sour cream over low to medium heat, stirring constantly, until chocolate is melted and mixture is smooth. Remove from heat and let cool to lukewarm.

MARBLED CHEESECAKE BARS

1 (18.25 ounce) yellow cake mix, with pudding in the mix, divided
4 eggs, divided
2 tablespoons vegetable oil
1 (8 ounce) package cream cheese, softened
½ cup sugar
1 ½ cups milk
1 teaspoon vanilla
2 (1 ounce squares) sweet baking chocolate, melted

Preheat oven to 325°. Reserve 1 cup dry cake mix. Set aside. Combine remaining cake mix, 1 egg and oil. Mix well (mixture will be crumbly). Using spatula press mixture firmly into bottom of a greased 9" x 13" baking pan.

In large bowl, beat cream cheese and sugar until light and fluffy. Add 3 eggs and reserved cake mix; blend well. Slowly add milk and vanilla, and beat on medium speed until smooth and thoroughly blended (about two minutes). Remove 1 cup of cream cheese mixture; pour remainder over batter in baking pan.

Add chocolate to reserved cream cheese mixture and blend well. Pour in zig zag fashion over cream cheese mixture in baking pan, and use butter knife to swirl, creating a marbled effect.

Bake for 50-55 minutes, until knife inserted into center comes out clean. Cool and refrigerate until serving.

CHERRY CHEESECAKE BARS

The sugar cookie mix makes a delicious, sweet crust for this cheesecake, which, by the way, is big enough for a hungry crowd.

1 (17.5 ounce) package sugar cookie mix, prepared
  as directed on package
1 (8 ounce) package cream cheese, softened
1 ½ cups milk
2 tablespoons sugar
½ teaspoon vanilla (clear)
1 (3.4 ounce) lemon flavor instant pudding mix
1 (20 ounce) can cherry pie filling

Preheat oven to 375°. Press cookie dough evenly into bottom of greased 9" x 13" baking pan. Bake for 15 minutes, until center is set and edges are browned. Remove from oven and let cool.

In medium bowl, beat cream cheese, milk, sugar and vanilla until mixture is smooth. Add pudding mix and beat on low speed about a minute, until mixture begins to thicken.

Spread mixture over cooled crust and refrigerate for at least 2 hours. Just before serving, spoon cherry pie filling over. Keep refrigerated.

MAPLE PECAN CHEESECAKE BARS

Crust
1 (22.3 ounce) sugar cookie mix
¾ cup chopped pecans
1 egg
½ cup (1 stick) butter or margarine, softened

Topping
2 (8 ounce) packages cream cheese, softened
1 cup packed brown sugar
2 tablespoons flour
2 eggs
2 teaspoons maple extract
¾ cup pecan halves
2 (1 ounce) squares sweetened chocolate, melted (for garnish)

Preheat oven to 350°. In medium bowl, blend cookie mix, pecans, egg and margarine until well blended. Press into bottom of greased 9" x 13" baking dish. Bake for 20 minutes. Remove from oven.

Reduce oven temperature to 325°. In large bowl, beat cream cheese and sugar until light and fluffy. Gradually add flour, then eggs and maple extract, mixing only until blended.

Pour mixture over warm crust, and arrange pecan halves attractively on surface. Place back in oven, and bake for 15 minutes.

Remove from oven and cool. Drizzle melted chocolate over. Cut into bars. Keep refrigerated.

PEANUT BUTTER BARS

1 (18.25 ounce) German chocolate cake mix
½ cup packed brown sugar
1 egg
¼ cup milk
2 tablespoons butter or margarine
½ cup peanut butter

Preheat oven to 325°. In large bowl, combine cake mix, sugar, egg, and milk.

Melt butter with peanut butter, and mix well. Add to cake mix ingredients in large bowl. Beat on low speed just enough to blend mixture. Press into bottom of greased and floured 9" x 13" baking pan. Bake for 25 to 30 minutes, or until cake tester comes out clean. Cool and frost with Peanut Butter Frosting.

Peanut Butter Frosting
2 tablespoons butter or margarine
2 tablespoons creamy peanut butter
3 tablespoons light corn syrup
1 teaspoon vanilla
1 cup semi-sweet chocolate chips
¼ cup powdered sugar

Heat butter, peanut butter, corn syrup and vanilla in a small saucepan over low heat, stirring frequently until mixture is smooth.

Remove from heat; stir in chocolate chips and beat until chocolate is melted and mixture is smooth. Add powdered sugar and blend well.

GOOEY SNICKERS BROWNIES

"Gooey" really describes these very dense, rich brownies.

1 (18.25 ounce) German chocolate cake mix
¾ cup butter or margarine, melted
½ cup evaporated milk
4 (2.07 ounce) Snickers candy bars, sliced
   in ⅛" slices

Preheat oven to 350°. In large bowl, combine cake mix, butter and evaporated milk. Beat on low speed until well-blended (1 to 2 minutes).

Spread half of batter into bottom of greased 9" x 13" baking pan. Bake for 10 minutes.

Remove from oven and place candy bar slices evenly over surface. Drop remaining half of batter by spoonful over candy bars, as evenly as possible.

Place back in oven and bake for 20 minutes (brownies will jiggle slightly on top when you remove them from oven). Let cool; cut into bars.

CARAMEL BROWNIES

1 (14 ounce) package caramels (about 45)
1 cup evaporated milk, divided
1 (18.25 ounce) Swiss chocolate cake mix
¾ cup butter or margarine, melted
1 cup semi-sweet chocolate chips
1 cup chopped pecans or walnuts

Preheat oven to 350°.

In large bowl, combine cake mix, butter and remaining ½ cup evaporated milk. Beat on low speed to blend. Spread half of batter into bottom of greased 9" x 13" baking pan.

Bake for 8 minutes. Remove from oven, and let cool slightly (about 15 minutes).

While cake is baking, in medium saucepan, melt caramels in ½ cup evaporated milk over low heat, stirring constantly until mixture is smooth. Remove from heat and set aside.

Sprinkle chocolate chips evenly over cake surface. Pour caramel mixture over chocolate chips, and sprinkle nuts over caramel. Drop remaining batter by spoonsful over nuts and caramel and swirl gently.

Return to oven for 18 to 20 minutes. Cool and then refrigerate at least 1 hour before serving.

MOUSSE-TOPPED BROWNIES

1 package brownie mix (for 8" x 8" size pan), batter
   prepared as directed on package
¾ cup heavy whipping cream
1 cup milk chocolate chips
3 eggs
⅓ cup butter

Preheat oven to 325°. Put brownie batter in greased
8" x 8" pan.

In small saucepan, heat whipping cream over
medium heat until hot, but not boiling. Stir in
chocolate chips and remove from heat. Stir until
chocolate is completely melted. Set aside.

In medium bowl, combine eggs and butter. Beat at
medium speed for several minutes (until eggs are
frothy). While continuing to beat, gradually add
chocolate mixture until well blended.

Pour chocolate mixture over brownie batter, and
bake for 45 to 50 minutes. Let cool completely, and
cut into bars.

COFFEE AND CREAM BROWNIES

1 (3 ounce) package cream cheese, softened
2 tablespoons butter or margarine, softened
¼ cup sugar
4 eggs, divided
½ teaspoon vanilla
1 tablespoon flour
2 tablespoons instant coffee granules
¼ cup warm water
1 (19.8 ounce) box family size brownie mix
½ cup vegetable oil

Preheat oven to 350°. Combine cream cheese and butter; blend thoroughly. Add sugar and blend until light and fluffy. Beat in 1 egg and vanilla, then stir in flour and mix well. Set aside.

In medium bowl, dissolve coffee in water. Add brownie mix, remaining eggs and vegetable oil; blend well. Pour half the batter into greased 9" x 13" baking dish.

Drop cheese mixture by heaping tablespoons over brownie batter. Pour remaining batter over cheese mixture and gently swirl a butter knife through it to create a marbled effect. Bake for 25 to 30 minutes.

BLACK FOREST CHERRY CAKE BROWNIES

It's hard to beat the flavor of chocolate and cherries. By cutting the cherries in half instead of chopping them, you can really taste the flavor when you bite into them.

1 box brownie mix (for 9" x 13" pan)
¼ cup maraschino cherry juice
½ cup vegetable oil
3 eggs
1 cup maraschino cherries, halved
¾ cup semi-sweet chocolate chips

Preheat oven to 350°. In medium bowl, combine brownie mix, maraschino cherry juice, oil and eggs until well blended. Gently stir in cherry halves and chocolate chips. Mix well. Pour batter into greased and floured 9" x 13" baking dish. Bake for 28 to 30 minutes. Cool, and frost with Cherry Icing.

Cherry Icing
6 tablespoons butter or margarine, softened
3 cups powdered sugar
⅛ teaspoon almond extract
¼ cup maraschino cherry juice

In medium bowl, cream butter and 1 cup of powdered sugar until well mixed. Add almond extract, then cherry juice and remaining sugar alternately, blending well after each addition, until icing is smooth and reaches frosting consistency.

MILKY WAY BROWNIES

1 (15.8 ounce) box brownie mix (for 8" x 8" pan)
3 (2.07 ounce) Milky Way candy bars, divided
5 tablespoons butter
1 teaspoon vanilla
¾ cup powdered sugar

Preheat oven to 350°. Mix brownies according to package directions. Pour half of batter into a greased 8" x 8" baking pan. Slice one of the Milky Way bars into pieces ⅛" thick. (Refrigerate candy bar beforehand to make it easier to slice.) Distribute candy bar slices evenly on batter. Cover with remaining batter, and smooth over. Bake for 40 to 42 minutes.

During the last 10 minutes of baking time, prepare the frosting. Chop the remaining two candy bars into 1" size chunks, and place in small saucepan. Add butter, and melt over low to medium heat, stirring constantly, until candy bars are completely melted and mixture is smooth. Lower heat to warm and stir in vanilla. Add powdered sugar a little at a time, stirring well with each addition. Frost brownies soon after removing from oven while still hot.

ROCKY ROAD BROWNIES

1 package brownie mix (for 9" x 13" pan)
1 cup mini marshmallows
1 (11.5 oz) package (2 cups) milk chocolate or
  semi-sweet chocolate chips
1 (14 ounce) can sweetened condensed milk
1 cup coarsely chopped pecans

Preheat oven to 350°. Prepare brownies as directed
on package for fudge-like brownies (use 2 eggs
instead of 3). Bake for 30 minutes.

Remove from oven and immediately sprinkle
marshmallows evenly over surface. Let cool.

In small saucepan, melt chocolate chips over low
heat. Remove from heat and stir in condensed milk.
Blend well. Stir in pecans. Pour evenly over
marshmallows. Let cool for several hours. Cut into
bars.

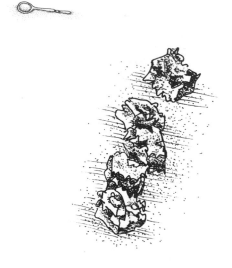

CRISPY-TOPPED BROWNIES

These brownies are so good! The brown sugar and coconut makes a crispy, tasty topping.

1 package brownie mix (for 9" x 13" pan), batter prepared according to package directions
¾ cup mini chocolate chips
3 tablespoons butter or margarine, melted
1 cup packed brown sugar
½ cup chopped nuts
1 cup shredded coconut

Preheat oven to 350°. Spread prepared batter in greased and floured 9" x 13" baking pan. Sprinkle chocolate chips evenly over surface.

In small bowl, combine butter, brown sugar, nuts and coconut; mix well. Sprinkle mixture over chocolate chips.

Bake for 25 to 30 minutes.

RASPBERRY ALMOND CHEESECAKE BROWNIES

1 package brownie mix (for 9" x 13" pan), batter
   prepared as directed on package
1 (12 ounce) can raspberry filling, divided
1 (8 ounce) package cream cheese, softened
2 tablespoons butter or margarine, softened
1 tablespoon cornstarch
1 (14 ounce) can sweetened condensed milk
1 egg
2 teaspoons almond extract

Prcheat oven to 350°. Prepare brownie batter as
directed on package. Add 1 cup raspberry filling to
the batter and beat on low speed until mixed. Pour
batter into greased and floured 9" x 13" baking pan.

In medium bowl, beat cream cheese, butter and
cornstarch until light and fluffy. While continuing to
beat, slowly add condensed milk, egg and almond
extract. Beat until well blended and smooth.

Pour cheese mixture over batter. Drop remaining
raspberry filling by spoonfuls evenly over cheese
mixture. Taking care not to over mix, swirl butter
knife or back of spoon gently through mixture to
create a marbled effect.

Bake for 40 to 45 minutes, or until lightly browned
on top. Cool and keep refrigerated.

CAPPUCCINO BROWNIES
WITH MOCHA ICING

3 tablespoons instant coffee granules
¼ cup warm water
1 package brownie mix (for 9" x 13" pan)
1 tablespoon cinnamon
3 eggs
½ cup vegetable oil

Preheat oven to 350°. Stir coffee into water until dissolved. In medium bowl, combine brownie mix, coffee mixture, cinnamon, eggs and oil.

Beat on low speed until blended. Pour batter into greased and floured 9" x 13" baking pan. Bake for 25 to 30 minutes. Cool and frost with Mocha Icing.

Mocha Icing
1 teaspoon instant coffee granules
¼ cup milk
4 ounces cream cheese, softened
1 (1 pound) package powdered sugar

Add coffee to milk and stir until dissolved.

In small bowl, beat cream cheese and coffee mixture until smooth and creamy.

Slowly add powdered sugar 1 cup at a time, beating well after each addition, until icing reaches frosting consistency.

Whip Up Some More . . .

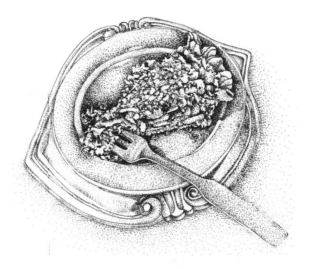

Here's the section where you'll find all the fabulous desserts that didn't quite fit into the cake, cookies, or bars categories. I've included an assortment of desserts, including pies, crunches, and various other delights. These recipes don't necessarily use a cake or cookie mix either. These use everything from gelatin and pudding mixes to flavored instant oatmeal (You've got to try the Cranberry Apple Crumb on page 247. It's absolutely one of my favorite and most popularly requested recipes).

PIÑA COLADA CHILLED PIE

This pie has an unbelievably smooth, creamy texture and tastes just like a Piña Colada. If you really like the taste of rum, splash a few extra tablespoons in for some added punch.

1 medium banana, thinly sliced
1 (9", 6 ounce) prepared graham cracker pie crust
2 (3.4 ounce) packages coconut cream flavor instant
   pudding mix
¾ cup coconut milk (not cream of coconut)
1 (8 ounce) can crushed pineapple with juice
⅓ cup rum
1 (8 ounce) container non-dairy whipped topping
¼ cup shredded coconut, for garnish

 Place banana slices in bottom of pie crust.

In large mixing bowl, combine pudding mix, coconut milk, pineapple, and rum. Blend on low speed until thoroughly mixed.

Fold in whipped topping and mix well. Pour mixture over bananas in pie crust, and sprinkle coconut over top, if desired.

You can generally find coconut milk in the Asian foods section of most grocery stores. I tried this recipe with regular milk, and it doesn't have the same texture or flavor. The coconut milk gives it a velvety, creamy texture and adds to the coconut flavor.

MOCHA S'MORES PIE

½ cup sour cream
1 cup milk chocolate chips
1 (9 ounce) prepared graham cracker pie crust
1 (14 ounce) can sweetened condensed milk
1 (8 ounce) package cream cheese, softened
2 tablespoons instant coffee granules
1 cup milk
1 (5.9 ounce) instant chocolate flavor pudding mix
   (6.5 servings size)
1 ½ cups marshmallow cream

In small saucepan, melt chocolate with sour cream over low to medium heat, stirring constantly until mixture is smooth and well blended. Pour into pie crust, and using back of spoon, smooth chocolate mixture evenly over bottom and sides of crust. Refrigerate to set chocolate while you prepare filling.

In medium mixing bowl, combine sweetened condensed milk and cream cheese. Blend on low speed. Dissolve coffee granules in milk, and add to cream cheese mixture while continuing to blend on low speed. While beating, slowly add pudding mix. Beat for 1 to 2 minutes. Pour mixture into pie shell and smooth top. Refrigerate until chilled (about 1 hour).

Heat marshmallow creme on half power in microwave to soften, and smooth over chocolate pie filling. Keep pie refrigerated until ready to serve.

Add the marshmallow creme topping just before serving or it will slide off of the pie as it sits.

MANDARIN ORANGE
AND CHOCOLATE PIE

This easy pie looks and tastes like orange sherbet. It makes a great summer dessert.

½ cup water
½ cup reserved orange syrup
1 (3 ounce) package orange flavor instant gelatin
1 ½ cups (1 pint) heavy whipping cream
1 cup sugar
1 (8 ounce) package cream cheese, softened
1 teaspoon vanilla
1 (1 ounce) square semi-sweet baking chocolate, melted and cooled
1 (9 ounce) prepared graham cracker pie crust
1 (11 ounce) can mandarin oranges in light syrup (drained, reserve ½ cup syrup)

In small pan, heat water and reserved orange syrup. Stir in gelatin until dissolved. Remove from heat and let cool.

Beat whip cream until peaks form; set aside.

Cream sugar, cream cheese, and vanilla. Pour gelatin mixture into cheese and sugar mixture, and blend well. Fold in whip cream.

(continued)

Remove 1 cup of this mixture and stir in chocolate. Pour into pie crust and smooth over.

Place in freezer for 10 to 15 minutes, or until firm. Gently stir oranges into remaining mixture; pour over chocolate. Refrigerate for several hours until firm (or until ready to serve).

For a decorative effect, beat remaining whipping cream with 1 tablespoon powdered sugar, and use for garnish.

CHOCOLATE PEANUT BUTTER PIE

¾ cup milk chocolate chips
4 tablespoons whipping cream
1 (3 ounce) package cream cheese, softened
½ cup creamy peanut butter
1 (4.6 ounce) vanilla pudding mix, cook and serve
  variety—not instant
1 ¾ cups milk
1 (9") prepared chocolate pie crust

In small saucepan, melt chocolate chips and cream over low heat; stirring until well-blended. Remove from heat.

In medium saucepan, combine cream cheese, peanut butter, vanilla pudding mix, and milk; bring to a boil, stirring frequently. Remove from heat and cool for 10 to 15 minutes.

Pour half of pudding mixture in pie crust and smooth over. Spread half of chocolate mixture over pudding and top with remaining pudding mixture. Using a butter knife, swirl chocolate through pudding mixture to create a marbled effect.

Take remaining chocolate and pour evenly over top. Let cool, and place pie in refrigerator until ready to serve.

TURTLE PIE

*This rich, wonderful pie combines the favorite flavors of chocolate
and caramel, just like the turtle candy.*

7 ounces individually wrapped caramels
  (about 22 pieces)
¼ cup evaporated milk
¾ cup chopped pecans, divided
2 (3 ounce) packages cream cheese, softened
½ cup (4 ounces) sour cream
1 ¼ cups milk
½ cup sugar
1 (3.9 ounce) package chocolate flavor instant
  pudding mix
1 (9") prepared graham cracker crust
½ cup chocolate syrup or fudge topping

In medium saucepan, combine caramels and
evaporated milk. Cook over medium heat for 5
minutes, stirring constantly. Remove from heat. Stir
in ½ cup pecans. Pour mixture into pie crust.

In a medium bowl, combine cream cheese, sour
cream, milk, and sugar. Blend until mixture is
smooth.

Add pudding mix, and blend for about 30 seconds
more, until pudding mix is well incorporated. Spoon
mixture over caramel in pie crust. Refrigerate for
about ½ hour, or until set.

Drizzle chocolate syrup, or spoon fudge topping, over
pie. Sprinkle with remaining pecans. Keep
refrigerated.

CHOCOLATE ALMOND PUDDING PIE

The pudding mix used in this pie and the versions that follow gives each its own unique flavor. These pies are very similar in nature to pecan pies; the nuts (and coconut) bake on the surface, making a thin crust over the pie filling beneath.

1 (3.9 ounce) chocolate flavor cook and serve pudding mix
1 cup light corn syrup
¾ cup evaporated milk
1 egg, slightly beaten
1 teaspoon almond extract
1 cup coarsely chopped pecans
1 (6 ounce) prepared chocolate pie shell

Preheat oven to 375°. In medium bowl, blend pudding mix with corn syrup. Gradually add evaporated milk, egg, and almond extract, stirring until well-blended.

Stir in pecans, and pour mixture into pie shell.

Bake for 40 minutes (just until top begins to crack). Remove from oven, and cool for several hours. (Pie will jiggle slightly in the middle when you remove from oven.) If desired, serve with a dollop of whipped cream.

(continued)

Variations
Coconut Pie
1 (3 ounce) vanilla flavor cook and serve pudding mix
1 cup light corn syrup
¾ cup evaporated milk
1 egg, slightly beaten
1 cup shredded coconut
1 (6 ounce) prepared graham cracker pie shell

Prepare as directed for Chocolate Almond Pudding Pie.

Cashew Toffee Pie
1 (3.9 oz) chocolate flavor cook and serve pudding mix
1 cup light corn syrup
¾ cup evaporated milk
1 egg, slightly beaten
¾ cup crushed toffee pieces (or crushed Heath or Skor bars)
½ cup coarsely chopped cashews
1 (9") prepared graham cracker pie shell

Prepare as directed for Chocolate Almond Pudding Pie and stir in toffee pieces and cashews.

APPLE CRUMB PIE

This pie is another family favorite; to save time I usually use a frozen pie shell.

5 to 7 medium Granny Smith apples
   (or other baking apple)
1 (6 ounce) unbaked pie shell
½ cup sugar
2 (1 ⅝ ounce) cinnamon and spice flavor instant
   oatmeal packets
½ cup finely chopped pecans
⅓ cup flour
⅓ cup packed brown sugar
⅓ cup butter, melted

Preheat oven to 400°. Pare apples and slice into eighths; arrange in unbaked pie shell. Sprinkle sugar evenly over apples.

In medium bowl, combine oatmeal, pecans, flour, and brown sugar; mix well. Add melted butter to mixture, and blend thoroughly (mixture should be crumbly).

Place mixture on top of apples, and bake for 35 to 40 minutes, or until top is browned.

CRANBERRY APPLE CRUMB

Although I usually serve this as a side dish, it works just as well as a dessert. It has been requested at family gatherings for years and is now a staple of our Thanksgiving and Christmas dinners. Be sure and buy extra packages of cranberries around the holidays when they're plentiful, and freeze them to enjoy this delicious dish throughout the year. (I just put the bagged cranberries in the freezer, and thaw them before using.)

4 cups Granny Smith apples (or other baking apple),
   peeled and chopped
2 cups fresh cranberries
2 tablespoons flour
1 cup sugar
3 (1 ⅝ ounce) cinnamon and spice flavor instant
   oatmeal packets
¾ cup chopped pecans
½ cup flour
½ cup packed brown sugar
½ cup butter, melted

Preheat oven to 350°. In large bowl, combine apples, cranberries, and 2 tablespoons flour. Toss to coat. Add sugar and mix well. Put mixture into ungreased 2 quart casserole dish.

Combine oatmeal, pecans, ½ cup remaining flour, brown sugar, and butter. Stir well, and spoon over apple mixture. Bake uncovered for 45 minutes or until topping is well browned.

AMARETTO PEACH CRUNCH

Like a peach pie with a crunchy topping (the cake mix and almonds form a crust over the pie filling as this bakes), the only way to enhance this dessert is to serve it with a big scoop of vanilla ice cream on the side.

2 (21 ounce) cans peach pie filling
½ cup Amaretto liqueur
1 (18.25 ounce) white cake mix
1 cup blanched, slivered almonds
½ cup (1 stick) butter or margarine

Preheat oven to 350°. Spread pie filling evenly in bottom of greased 9" x 13" baking pan. Pour Amaretto over filling.

Sprinkle cake mix evenly over all and smooth top. Sprinkle almonds evenly over cake mix.

Slice butter into ⅛" slices and place over entire surface. Bake for 40-45 minutes, until top is nicely browned.

BLUEBERRY CRUNCH

It's pretty hard to visualize how this dish will turn out until you make it yourself. (This version was a big hit with my husband's co-workers.) If you like the taste of blueberry, you'll love this dessert.

1 (20 ounce) can crushed pineapple with juice
½ cup packed brown sugar
1 teaspoon cinnamon
1 (21 ounce) can blueberry pie filling
1 (18.25 ounce) yellow cake mix
1 cup chopped pecans
½ cup (1 stick) butter or margarine

Preheat oven to 350°. Grease 9" x 13" baking pan. Pour pineapple and juice into pan; spread evenly. Sprinkle brown sugar and cinnamon over.

Drop blueberry pie filling over pineapple, and smooth over gently.

Sprinkle cake mix evenly over pie filling, and sprinkle pecans over cake mix. Slice butter into ⅛" pieces and distribute over surface. Bake for 50 to 55 minutes, or until lightly browned on top.

BANANA CREAM DELIGHT

¾ cup (1 ½ sticks) butter or margarine
1 ½ cups flour
⅔ cup finely ground walnuts
1 (8 ounce) package cream cheese, softened
1 cup powdered sugar
1 (8 ounce) container frozen whipped topping (evenly
   divided)
3 cups milk
2 (3.4 ounce) packages banana cream flavor instant
   pudding
2 bananas

Preheat oven to 350°. In medium bowl, cream
margarine and flour. Add walnuts, and blend
thoroughly. Press into the bottom of an ungreased
9" x 13" baking dish. Bake for 30 minutes. Let cool.

Mix cream cheese with powdered sugar, then add 4
ounces frozen topping, and blend. Spread mixture
over cooled crust. In medium bowl, whisk milk and
pudding mix for 2 minutes. Pour over cheese
mixture.

Slice bananas and place on top of pudding. Carefully
spread remaining 4 ounces frozen whipped topping
over all. Refrigerate for several hours before serving.

SPICY APPLE TART

This dish is not only tasty, but also very pretty. The apples and custard-like filling make an attractive topping for the spicy, sweet base.

1 (18.25 ounce) spice cake mix
½ cup chopped walnuts
½ cup (1 stick) butter or margarine, softened
¼ cup, plus 2 tablespoons sugar, divided
1 teaspoon cinnamon
1 cup sour cream
1 egg
3 Granny Smith or baking apples, peeled, cored, and thinly sliced
½ cup chopped dates

Preheat oven to 350°. In large bowl, combine cake mix, walnuts, and butter. Blend on low speed until butter is thoroughly incorporated (mixture will be crumbly). Press mixture into bottom and ¼ of the way up the sides of greased and floured 9" x 13" baking pan. Bake for 10 minutes.

While crust is baking, in small bowl mix cinnamon with ¼ cup sugar until well-blended. Set aside.

In a separate bowl, blend sour cream with egg and remaining 2 tablespoons sugar.

Remove crust from oven. Distribute apple slices and dates evenly over bottom. Sprinkle cinnamon-sugar mixture over. Spoon sour cream mixture on top. Bake for 35 to 40 minutes.

TWO-TONED CHOCOLATE CHEESECAKE

You can eat this cheesecake as is (it just melts in your mouth) or spoon some cherry pie filling or strawberries in syrup over each slice just before serving. It's a really pretty dessert; the darker chocolate cheesecake layer contrasts with the white cheesecake layer beneath, which sits atop a cookie-like crust.

1 (18.25 ounce) yellow cake mix
¼ cup vegetable oil
3 eggs, divided
1 ¼ cups milk chocolate chips, divided
3 (8 ounce) packages cream cheese, softened
½ cup sugar
½ cup sour cream
½ cup whipping cream

Preheat oven to 350°. Reserve 1 cup dry cake mix and set aside.

To prepare crust, put remaining cake mix, oil, and 1 egg in large bowl. Beat on low speed until dough forms.

Add ½ cup chocolate chips and blend into mixture.

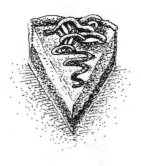

(continued)

🥄 Press dough into bottom of greased and floured 9" x 13" baking pan. Bake for 10 minutes.

🥄 While crust is baking, prepare cheesecake filling. In large bowl (the same one you made the crust in is fine), beat cream cheese until smooth and creamy. Add 2 eggs, one at a time, beating well after each addition.

🥄 Add reserved cake mix, sugar, sour cream, and whipping cream. Beat on low speed to blend, then beat on medium speed for 3 minutes, until mixture is light and fluffy.

🥄 Reserve 2 cups of cheese mixture, and spoon remaining mixture over hot, baked crust. Melt remaining ¾ cup chocolate chips, and blend into reserved cheese mixture. Spoon chocolate cheese mixture carefully over cheese mixture in pan.

🥄 Bake for 30 to 35 minutes, until edges are set. Don't overcook. Cool to room temperature and then refrigerate before serving.

BANANA CHOCOLATE TREAT

1 (18.25 ounce) yellow cake mix
½ cup (1 stick) butter or margarine, softened
2 cups semi-sweet chocolate chips
4 cups milk, divided
4 ½ cups mini marshmallows, divided
2 large bananas, sliced
2 (3.4 ounce) packages vanilla flavor instant pudding
   mix
1 cup frozen whipped topping, thawed
1 ½ cups shredded coconut, divided

Preheat oven to 350°. In large bowl, combine cake mix with butter; blend until mixture is crumbly. Press into bottom of a greased 9" x 13" baking dish. Bake for 10 minutes. Remove from oven and let cool.

In large saucepan, combine chocolate chips, 1 cup milk, and 2 cups marshmallows. Cook over low heat, stirring constantly until marshmallows are melted. Pour mixture over cooled crust. Chill for about an hour.

Place banana slices in single layer over chocolate mixture.

In medium bowl, whisk pudding mix with 3 cups milk. Whisk in whipped topping. Stir in remaining marshmallows and 1 cup coconut. Spoon over bananas. Sprinkle ½ cup coconut over. Keep refrigerated.

PISTACHIO MARSHMALLOW SALAD

With its pale green color, this salad adds a nice touch of color to any meal. (I always think it looks festive next to the red color of cranberry sauce around the holidays. But it also works well throughout the year used as either a dessert or side dish.)

1 (3.4 ounce) package pistachio flavor instant pudding mix
1 (8 ounce) container frozen whipped topping
1 (20 ounce) can crushed pineapple with juice
1 cup chopped pecans
1 ½ cups miniature marshmallows
½ cup shredded coconut (optional)

In large bowl, combine pudding mix and whipped topping; stir until well blended. Add pineapple, pecans, marshmallows, and coconut (if desired). Stir well. Refrigerate until ready to serve.

FUN FUDGE SHAPES

This is a fun and EASY candy recipe that uses pudding mix as a basic ingredient. It's a great way to make special holiday-shaped candies using mini cake pans. You can whip up a batch in less than 10 minutes, and have them ready to serve within the next hour.

½ cup (1 stick) butter or margarine
½ cup milk
2 (3.4 ounce) packages chocolate cook and serve
   pudding mix (not instant)
1 (1 pound) box powdered sugar
1 cup mini marshmallows
½ cup chopped pecans

In heavy, medium saucepan, combine butter, milk, and pudding mix. Heat to a simmer and cook for 2 minutes, stirring constantly.

Remove from heat and stir in powdered sugar until well blended, then stir in marshmallows and pecans.

Spoon mixture into greased mini cake pan (I especially like using pans with holiday shapes. For instance, around Valentine's Day, I like to use a pan that has six small heart shapes. Each are a few inches wide and about 1 ¼" deep. This recipe is enough to make six of them.)

Refrigerate until firm. Turn out of pan and serve.

CHUNKY CHOCOLATE CANDY

1 (3.4 ounce) package chocolate cook and serve
   pudding mix (not instant)
1 cup sugar
½ cup packed brown sugar
½ cup evaporated milk
1 tablespoon butter or margarine
1 cup chopped pecans (or other nuts)
½ cup shredded coconut
½ cup raisins

In heavy medium saucepan, combine pudding mix, sugar, brown sugar, milk, and butter. Cook over medium heat until sugar dissolves and mixture comes to a boil.

Continue cooking, stirring frequently, until mixture reaches the softball stage (237° F) on a candy thermometer (about 7 minutes).

Remove from heat and stir in pecans, coconut, and raisins. Beat well and before mixture starts to harden (you need to work fast), drop by heaping spoonsful onto waxed paper.

FESTIVE PUMPKIN TREAT

1 (17.5 ounce) oatmeal cookie mix, prepared as
   directed on package
1 (8 ounce) package cream cheese, softened
2 tablespoons orange liqueur (or milk)
2 tablespoons sugar
2 cups frozen whipped topping, thawed
1 cup cold milk
1 (16 ounce) can pumpkin
2 (3.4 ounce) packages vanilla flavor instant pudding
mix
1 teaspoon cinnamon
¼ teaspoon ground ginger
⅛ teaspoon (pinch) ground cloves

Topping (optional)
½ cup chopped pecans (or other nuts)
2 tablespoons butter or margarine
⅓ cup packed brown sugar

Preheat oven to 375°. Press cookie batter into
bottom of greased 9" x 13" baking pan. Bake for 10
to 12 minutes, or until lightly browned. Remove from
oven and cool.

While cookie crust is baking, prepare toppings. In
medium bowl, combine cream cheese with orange
liqueur and sugar. Beat on medium until mixture is
smooth. Fold in whipped topping. Set aside.

In large bowl, combine milk with pumpkin, pudding
mixes, cinnamon, ginger, and cloves. Beat with
whisk until well blended.

(continued)

Spread pumpkin mixture over cooled crust and smooth over top. Carefully cover with cream cheese mixture and smooth over.

If you want to serve this with the topping: in small bowl mix pecans, butter and brown sugar. Sprinkle over slices just before serving.

This sets up fairly quickly, but for best results, refrigerate for several hours.

Several recipes throughout this book are perfect for one holiday or another. Sometimes I've pointed this out in the recipes, but I by no means covered them all. So, to make it easy to see all of the recipes that would be especially good for one holiday or another, we've listed them here in this handy chart.

Valentine's Day
Strawberry Bundt Cake, p. 94
Red Velvet Cake, p. 117
Strawberry Cream Cheese Bars, p. 218
Black Forest Cherry Cake Brownies, p. 231
Black Forest Cherry Cookies, p. 174
Valentine's Day Cheery-Cherry Cookies, p. 185

St. Patrick's Day
Key Lime Pie Cake, p. 42
Watergate Cake, p. 88
Pina Colada Chilled Pie, p. 238
Pistachio Marshmallow Salad, p. 255

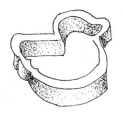

Easter
Anisette Easter Cake, p. 68
Pretty Pastel Easter Cookies, p. 185
Pistachio Marshmallow Salad, p. 255

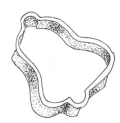

Fourth of July
Watermelon Cake
    with Lime Frosting, p. 119
Blueberry Crunch, p. 249

AT A GLANCE

Halloween
Halloween Orange
  and Chocolate Cookies, p. 184
Mandarin Orange and Chocolate Pie, p. 240

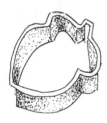

Thanksgiving
Pumpkin Rum Cake, p. 62
Date Spice Cake
  with Brown Sugar Glaze, p. 85
Autumn Spice Cake, p. 108
Pumpkin Bars, p. 208
Maple Pecan Cheesecake Bars, p. 225
Molasses Spice Cookies, p. 159
Maple Iced Walnut Cookies, p. 176
Spicy Apple Tart, p. 251

Christmas
Colossal Petits Fours, p. 138
Cherry Cake, p. 118
Spicy Mincemeat Cookies, p. 153
Holiday Fruitcake Cookies, p. 153
Ginger Jam Sandwich Cookies, p. 180
Peppermint Christmas Cookies, p. 184
Gingerbread Rolled Cookies, p. 190
Cranberry Apple Crumb, p. 247

TERMS YOU'LL WANT TO KNOW
(Tools and Terminology)

Baking Pans

The baking pans used for the cake recipes in this book are mostly limited to the following three: rectangular baking pan, round cake pans, and Bundt pan.

Round cake pans come in a couple of different sizes and materials. The ones used for making the recipes in this book were 8 ¼" x 2" glass pans. Glass and dark-colored pans absorb more heat than shiny metal ones, which makes the cakes brown more quickly, so you'll need to take this into account when using your own. You may need to extend the cooking time slightly if you're using metal pans.

Some other common sizes are 8" x 1 ½", 9" x 1 ½", and 9" x 2". For the recipes in this book, a 9" x 1 ½" or 9" x 2" would work just fine.

Rectangular baking pans come in several different sizes also, but the one used in this book was a 13" x 9" x 2" metal pan, which is probably the most common. If you're using a larger size, you'll want to check the cake for doneness a few minutes before the cooking time specified in the recipe to make sure your cake isn't over baking. You'll also want to check a little earlier if you're using a glass pan, since glass pans make the baked good cook faster.

Bundt Pan—A traditional Bundt pan is 10"wide, 3 ½" deep and holds 12 cups. The hole in the middle of this tube pan with fluted sides provides for even heating and cooking.

Beat

When the recipe says to "beat" the ingredients, you can do this with an electric mixer (usually set to medium speed) or by hand. 100 strokes by hand roughly equals 1 minute by electric mixer.

Cream

To cream ingredients means to beat them until the mixture is soft, smooth and "creamy." Frequently a recipe will specify creaming butter and sugar or cream cheese and sugar. When creaming two or more ingredients together, you want the end result to be a uniformly smooth mixture, where none of the individual ingredients are identifiable anymore.

Depending upon the quantity of ingredients that needs to be blended, I usually use a fork for small quantities and an electric mixer for larger batches.

Cut-in

Cutting-in ingredients refers to the way you mix butter with dry ingredients, using a knife or pastry blender, until the mixture is crumbly. You'll use this technique when making the crumb toppings called for in several recipes in this book.

Fold

Folding an ingredient into a recipe is done when you're combining a light, airy mixture (like beaten egg whites) with a heavier mixture (such as cake batter).

To do this, place the lighter mixture on top of the heavier one in a large bowl. Then, starting at the back of the bowl, use a rubber spatula to cut down vertically through the two mixtures, across the bottom of the bowl and up the nearest side. Rotate the bowl slightly with each series of strokes. You should use a gentle motion, and continue until the mixtures are combined.

Double Boiler

Used in recipes that need indirect, gentle heat to melt ingredients or cook some frostings (like 7 Minute Frosting). A double boiler is made up of two pots—one is designed to fit snugly over the other, leaving enough room to put several inches of water in the bottom. If you don't have a double boiler, you can easily make one by putting a large metal bowl over a pot of simmering water, without letting the water touch the bowl.

Greasing and Flouring

Greasing and flouring your cake pans is critical for successful baking. You don't want half of your cake to stick to the pan when you go to turn it out onto a serving tray. For best results, use solid shortening (like Crisco). Using a small piece of waxed paper or paper towel, spread a thin layer of shortening over the entire interior surface of the pan.

Then dust it by placing about a tablespoon of flour inside and shaking it around until the entire surface is coated. Dump out the remaining flour and fill the pan with batter.

Jelly Roll Pan

Jelly roll pans are shallow, rectangular baking pans with 1" sides (much like a cookie sheet). They come in several sizes, but the most common is 15 ½" x 10 ½" x 1". They are used, as the name implies, for making jelly rolls as well as cakes and some bars. This is the pan used in the Colossal Petits Fours recipe in this book because of its shallow depth, which makes a cake just the right height for cutting with a cookie cutter.

Pastry Blender

This useful tool is designed for cutting butter or margarine into flour (or a flour mixture). It's fitted with five or six U-shaped, rigid, curved wires and easily slices butter into small pieces (without melting it) to mix with the flour. You'll want to have this for recipes that require a crumb topping (like Cranberry Apple Crumb).

Separating Eggs

When you separate eggs, you want to cleanly remove the yolk from the white. There are a couple of methods for doing this:

1) Method One—Take a dry egg in your hand and tap it firmly across the wide end of the shell, on the rim of the bowl.

   Then, holding the widest part in your hand, pull the shells apart. The widest end becomes the "cup" that will hold the yolk, as the white drips into the bowl.

   Pour the yolk into the other shell, continuing to let the white drip into the bowl, and repeat until all the white is removed and the yolk is left. Dump the yolk into another bowl or container.

   Inspect the whites to be sure that no shell fragments fell in with them.

2) Method 2—use a yolk separator, which is designed for this purpose. (I frankly haven't used a yolk separator, but believe if you want to take extra precautions with regard to minimizing the risk of contamination from salmonella germs on the shells, you may want to use one. Since the eggs used in the cake batter are cooked, I don't think it's necessary to worry about it though.)

Did You Know? Cold eggs separate easier
than those at room temperature.

Spatula

A spatula is a flat, narrow utensil, made from plastic or metal, that comes in several sizes and is used for spreading icings. In this book, I've referred to it as an "icing spatula" to distinguish it from a rubber scraper, also called a spatula.

A rubber scraper (spatula) is great for scraping liquid ingredients and batters out of bowls and utensils. It helps ensure that all of your ingredient goes into the recipe or pan (and also makes cleanup easier too).

A turner, also frequently called a spatula, is what you typically use to flip pancakes. These are also used to lift cookies from a baking sheet. They come in both metal and plastic; if you're using non-stick cookie sheets, you'll want to be sure and use a plastic spatula/turner so you don't scratch the surface of your pan.

Whisk

A wire whisk consists of a series of looped wires fastened at the top by a long handle. They are used to whip air into ingredients such as egg whites or whipping cream. They're also great for getting a smooth consistency in some icing recipes. They come in many sizes, and it's useful to have a couple. I have a very small one and a large one and use both all the time.

YOUR INGREDIENTS

BUTTER

Made from churned cream, butter by law is at least 80% milk fat, with water and some milk solids making up the remaining 20%.

Storage
Butter should be its stored in the refrigerator and covered, since it picks up other food flavors. (Don't store it next to foods with strong odors like onions or garlic.) You can keep it for up to two weeks, but should use it before the expiration date printed on the package.

You can also freeze butter for up to four months. Seal it in a plastic bag for best results.

Substitutions
If necessary, you can use unsalted butter instead of salted (or vice versa) if that's what you have on hand. You don't need to worry about adding additional salt to your recipe if you use unsalted.

Whipped butter can be used in the place of stick butter as well, but be sure to substitute the amount you need by weight, not volume. For example, if the recipe requires 1 cup (2 sticks) of butter (which is half a pound), you'll want to use 8 ounces of whipped butter.

You can also use margarine as a substitute for butter, although it won't provide the same rich flavor that butter does.

Usage
Cutting-In Butter

When a recipe says to "cut-in butter," this means to mix cold butter with the other ingredients by gently pressing a pastry blender or cutter into the butter and flour mixture until the mixture is crumbly and looks like coarse meal.

If you don't have a pastry blender you can use two knives with the blades close together to "saw" through the ingredients, or use a fork to break it into small pieces.

Creaming

When a recipes calls for "creaming the butter," it means to beat the butter until it's soft, smooth and creamy. You can do this by hand, with a food processor, or with an electric hand mixer. It's much easier to do this if the butter is at room temperature and not cold.

CHOCOLATE

My favorite ingredient! Chocolate is made from cocoa beans which are process to obtain cocoa butter and a dark brown paste called "liquor." Once dried, the liquor is ground into the powder known as unsweetened cocoa.

Chocolate comes in many forms: bars, chips, chunks, cocoa powder, etc., and it's helpful to know a little about the ones that may be called for in a recipe. Here's a rundown of the most commonly-used forms you'll see required for recipes in this book:

- Unsweetened baking chocolate, frequently used as bars or squares, contains chocolate liquor (the substance extracted from the hulled beans) and between 50% and 58% cocoa butter.

- Bittersweet chocolate, usually called for in squares or bars, contains at least 35% chocolate liquor, sugar and vanilla.

- Semisweet and sweet chocolate, which comes in baking chips, bars, or squares, contains between 15 and 35% chocolate liquor, sugar and vanilla.

- Milk chocolate, frequently called for as chips or squares, contains 10% chocolate liquor, sugar, vanilla and at least 12% milk solids.

- Unsweetened cocoa is cocoa liquor that has been dried and ground into powder.

   Did You Know? White chocolate is not "true chocolate" because it contains no chocolate liquor, but is instead prepared from sugar, cocoa butter, milk solids and vanilla.

Storage

Keep chocolate stored tightly wrapped in a plastic bag in a cool, dry location. The ideal storage temperature is around 75 degrees. If chocolate has been stored at a high temperature, it may turn grayish (this is called "bloom" and is a result of the fat content surfacing). Go ahead and use it anyway. This discoloration is perfectly harmless.

Unsweetened, bittersweet, and semisweet chocolate, if properly stored, can stay fresh for very long periods of time.

Unsweetened dry cocoa powder will keep indefinitely if stored in a cool, dry location.

Don't store milk chocolate and white chocolate for longer than nine months, because they contain milk solids.

Substitutions

You can use bittersweet and semisweet chocolate interchangeably in recipes, but you may notice some slight differences in flavor and texture.

If you don't have unsweetened cocoa but do have Dutch-processed cocoa, you can go ahead and use it instead, although the flavor will be milder.

1 ounce semisweet chocolate = 3 tablespoons semisweet chocolate pieces or 1 ounce unsweetened chocolate plus 1 tablespoon sugar.

1 ounce unsweetened chocolate = 3 tablespoons unsweetened cocoa, plus 1 tablespoon melted butter.

1 ounce sweet baking chocolate= 2 tablespoons unsweetened cocoa, plus 4 teaspoons sugar and 2 teaspoons butter.

Substitution "Don'ts"

Don't use chocolate syrup in the place of melted chocolate. (Use it only when specifically called for.)

Instant cocoa mix is not the same as unsweetened cocoa. It contains milk powder and sugar and may affect the flavor of your baked goods.

Usage

Melting chocolate: Melt chocolate in the microwave, over direct heat, or over hot water.

To microwave: Use a microwave-safe bowl and set the power to medium (or half-power), and heat for short periods of time (30 to 45 seconds) stirring occasionally until chocolate is melted.

To melt over direct heat: Place chocolate in pan over very low heat. Be careful when melting over direct heat, as chocolate scorches easily. You'll want to heat it very slowly and stir it frequently.

To melt over hot water (using a double boiler) heat the chocolate slowly over hot, not boiling, water (as steam can stiffen or harden it).

Note: Be sure to cool the melted chocolate to about 80 degrees before adding it to your recipe.

Did You Know? Chocolate comes from cocoa beans that grow in pods on a tropical "Theobroma cacao" tree, cultivated mainly in South American countries.

EGGS

Eggs are used to not only add flavor and color, but also to tenderize and provide structure for your baked goods. Both brown and white eggs contain the same flavor and nutritional value.

Storage

Eggs should always be refrigerated and stored in their original carton, if possible, which will help keep them from absorbing refrigerator odors.

You can store eggs for up to five weeks beyond the packing or expiration date on the carton, as long as they are not cracked or broken.

Substitutions

There are some substitutions that can be made for eggs:

1 whole egg = 2 egg whites. (Be aware that they won't provide the same flavor and texture, however.)

¼ cup liquid egg substitute = 1 whole egg. Egg substitutes contain egg whites, nonfat milk, vegetable oils and other ingredients to replace the yolk. If you use egg substitutes in a cake recipe, for example, your end result may not be as tender or rich.

1 egg white = 1 tablespoons meringue powder plus 2 tablespoons water. You can use powdered egg whites in most recipes that call for egg whites.

Usage
Beating egg whites

For best results, when beating egg whites, make sure that no traces of broken yolk have gotten into the whites. Make sure your bowl and beaters don't have any traces of fat on them, which can prevent the whites from expanding to their full volume when beaten. (To ensure you don't have any fat on the utensils, you can rinse them in a solution of water and some vinegar.)

It's best to bring egg whites to room temperature for 20 minutes after you've separated them from the yolks. This will help the egg whites beat to their highest volume.

Select clean, fresh eggs which have been handled properly and refrigerated.

Don't use cracked or leaking eggs that may have a bad odor or unnatural color when cracked open. They may have been contaminated with salmonella, and it's better not to take the chance.

Use large eggs unless a recipe specifies a different size.

Cold eggs are easiest to separate.

Did You Know? You can easily test an egg for freshness by placing it in a bowl deep enough to cover be able to cover it with water (which should be cold). If the egg stays on the bottom of the bowl, it's fresh. If it stands up and bobs on the bottom, it isn't as fresh. If it floats, you need to throw it away!

Here's a little information about the different kinds of milk products called for in cake and icing recipes:

- Whole milk has had no fat removed and contains 3 ½% milk fat.
- Buttermilk traditionally was the liquid remaining after butter was churned. Today it is made by adding a culture to low-fat or non-fat milk, which gives it a thick texture and tangy flavor.
- Half-and-half is a mixture of milk and cream and contains between 10.5% and 18% milk fat.
- Evaporated milk is milk that has had 60% of its water removed.
- Sweetened condensed milk has 50% of the water removed. The remaining mixture is 40% sugar and very sticky and sweet.
- Whipping Cream is skimmed from milk that has been standing 24 hours or longer. It's usually classified as either light, meaning it has 30 to 36% milkfat, or heavy, meaning it contains from 36% to 40% milkfat.
- Half-and-half is a mixture of milk and cream that contains about 10% to 18% milkfat.

Storage

Store milk products in their original containers in the refrigerator at a temperature of 35° to 40° F.

You can store unopened cans of evaporated milk or sweetened condensed milk at room temperature for up to 12 months. Once you open it, however, refrigerate the unused portion in an airtight container for up to five days.

It's best not to freeze milk, cream, buttermilk, evaporated milk or sweetened condensed milk because the texture will be affected.

Substitutions

Whole milk, reduced fat and fat free milk can be used interchangeably in recipes.

1 cup buttermilk = 1 tablespoon vinegar or lemon juice in a measuring cup with enough milk to equal 1 cup. Let stand 5 minutes before using.

1 cup refrigerated fresh milk = ½ cup evaporated milk, plus ½ cup water.

1 cup whipping cream = ¾ cup milk and ⅓ cup butter. (Don't use this for to make whipped cream; use only for baking.)

One 14-ounce can sweetened condensed milk = 1 cup instant nonfat dry milk, ⅔ cup granulated sugar, ½ cup boiling water and 3 tablespoons melted butter. Beat in a blender or food processor until smooth.

Substitution Don'ts

Don't use evaporated milk in place of sweetened condensed milk.

NUTS

Nuts add flavor and a crunchy texture to baked products. They are actually the edible kernel of a dried fruit contained inside a hard shell. The most commonly-used nuts called for in recipes within this book include walnuts, pecans, and almonds.

You can either purchase them chopped or whole, or still within the shells to shell them yourself.
Most of the recipes will specify chopped or ground nuts. If you're buying them already chopped, be aware that 1 cup chopped nuts equals 4 ounces.

Storage
Store shelled nuts in an airtight container in a cool place. Because of their high fat content, nuts can go rancid very quickly. Heat, light and moisture also make nuts go rancid faster.

You can refrigerate shelled nuts for up to 4 months, or freeze them for up to 6. Unshelled nuts can be kept about twice as long.

Substitutions
Often you can substitute the same quantity of a different nut than called for in the recipe with perfectly fine results.

Usage
When you choose shelled nuts, look for those that are crisp in texture and uniform in color. Don't buy them if they are shriveled or discolored. To be sure they are fresh before you use them, it's always best to taste them before adding them to your recipe.

OATS

Oats add a chewy texture and a nutty flavor to baked products. You'll notice that there are several kinds of dried oats on the market:

Old-Fashioned: The entire oat kernel is rolled to make old-fashioned rolled oats.

Quick-Cooking: The oat kernel is cut into pieces before being rolled thinly to make quick-cooking oats.

Instant Oatmeal: The oats are cut very fine and processed so that no cooking is necessary, other than adding boiling water. Instant oatmeal is often flavored with sugar and spices.

Storage

Store oats in a cool dry place in a tightly covered container, to keep out dust, moisture and insects, for up to six months.

You can also freeze oats for up to one year in a plastic freezer bag.

Although they don't go bad, oats may become stale with age.

Substitutions

Old-fashioned and quick-cooking oats can be used interchangeably.

Do not, however, use instant oatmeal the place of either old-fashioned or quick-cooking oats. Because it usually contains sugar and other flavors, instant oatmeal can alter the texture and taste of your recipe.

SPICES

Spices, which are obtained from the bark, buds, fruit, roots, seeds or stems of a variety of plants (as opposed to herbs, which are harvested mainly from the leafy parts of plants) have been prized for centuries for their pungent aroma and ability to flavor foods.

Many popular baking spices include allspice, cardamom, cinnamon, cloves, ginger, and nutmeg, which are available both in whole or ground form. The recipes in this book all use ground spices.

Storage
Spices should be stored in airtight containers in a cool, dark location for about 6 months. When exposed to heat, light, and moisture, spices can lose their flavor more quickly. Do not store spices above the range or oven.

Substitutions
1 teaspoon ground allspice = ¼ teaspoon ground cinnamon, ½ teaspoon ground cloves and ¼ teaspoon ground nutmeg, mixed together.

1 teaspoon ground cinnamon: ½ teaspoon ground allspice or 1 teaspoon ground cardamom.

1 teaspoon ground ginger = ½ teaspoon ground mace + ½ teaspoon grated lemon peel.

1 teaspoon ground nutmeg = 1 teaspoon ground allspice or 1 teaspoon ground cloves or 1 teaspoon ground mace.

Usage
Because they quickly lose their aroma and flavor, it's best to buy ground spices in small amounts.

SUGAR

In addition to adding sweetness, sugar also tenderizes and helps baked goods to brown.

Granulated white sugar is refined cane or beet sugar. It's what's intended in all the recipes that don't specify a particular type of sugar (e.g., brown sugar or powdered sugar).

Powdered (or confectioner's) sugar is granulated sugar that has been ground to a fine powder and had cornstarch added to prevent it from clumping. It provides smoothness for recipes, such as those for icings, where granulated sugar would be too grainy.

Brown sugar is granulated sugar with molasses added to it and it comes in two types. Light brown sugar has a more delicate flavor than its counterpart dark brown sugar. Unless dark brown sugar is specified in the recipe, use light brown sugar. (Although you're probably safe using either for most of the recipes in this book.)

Storage
Store granulated sugar tightly covered in a cool, dry location. (A moist location, like a refrigerator, can encourage clumping.)

Brown sugar and powdered sugar should be stored in either a plastic bag or airtight container.

Although sugars don't go bad, they can sometime harden or form lumps when exposed to moisture.

Substitutions
1 cup granulated sugar = ¾ cup honey (you must also reduce the liquid in the recipe by ¼ cup).

1 cup granulated sugar = ½ cup corn syrup.

1 cup powdered sugar = 1 cup granulated sugar plus ⅛ teaspoon cornstarch (process on high speed in a food processor until it has a fine texture).

1 cup light brown sugar = 1 cup granulated sugar plus 2 tablespoons molasses.

Usage

Here are a few tips for properly measuring your sugar, to ensure best results:

Granulated sugar: Spoon the sugar into a measuring cup and level with a spatula or knife.

Powdered sugar: Lightly spoon sugar into dry measuring cup and level top with a spatula or knife.

Brown sugar: Pack brown sugar firmly into a dry measuring cup.

Did You Know? To soften brown sugar that has hardened you can do one of two things:

1) Put the sugar in a container, cover with a piece of foil or plastic wrap, and place a crumpled, damp paper towel on the foil or wrap. Cover tightly and let sit. (The sugar will absorb the moisture from the paper towel and become soft.)

2) The faster method: Put an open bag of brown sugar in the microwave and set 1 cup of water next to it. Microwave on high power (100%) for 2 to 3 minutes, stopping frequently to check your progress, until brown sugar is softened.

VANILLA EXTRACT

Vanilla extract adds a very sweet, fragrant flavor to baked goods. It is produced from the long, thin pods harvested from an orchid native to tropical America. It has been cultivated and processed for hundreds of years.

Vanilla extract is produced by processing vanilla beans in an alcohol and water mixture and then aging it for several months.

Storage
Store vanilla extract in a cool, dark place, with the bottle tightly closed, to prevent evaporation and loss of flavor. Vanilla extract will stay fresh for years if stored properly.

Substitutions
You can use imitation vanilla in the place of real vanilla extract, as is sometimes necessary with certain recipes, although it's not optimal. It doesn't have the same flavor, and the imitation vanilla can actually have an artificial taste.

Some of the recipes in this book call for using imitation vanilla when real vanilla would discolor the end result (for instance, in a white, sugar glaze). If the recipe doesn't specify "clear" vanilla, use the real thing!

Usage
When measuring vanilla, it's a good idea not to measure over your mixing bowl to avoid accidentally spilling more than you need into your recipe.

YEAST

Yeast is a living, plant-like, single-cell microscopic organism that is activated by warm liquid. As it feeds on sugar or starch it grows and multiplies, releasing carbon dioxide as it grows, the gas that causes baked products to rise and produces a light texture in the finished bread product.

There are several forms of yeast on the market:
- Active dry yeast, the most popular form, is sold as dry granules in .25 ounce packets or 4 ounce jars. The recipes in this book call for the .25 ounce packets, although you can use the equivalent amount measured from the jar (see "Substitutions" below).
- Quick-rising yeast is a more active strain of yeast than regular active dry yeast and can reduce the rising time by one-third.
- Compressed fresh yeast is a small block or "cake" of moist yeast found in the refrigerated section of the supermarket. It is very perishable and should be used within a week or two of purchase or by the expiration date printed on the package.

Storage
Packets of dry yeast and quick-rising yeast need to be stored in cool, dry location to keep out moisture. Once opened, however, it's best to store jars of yeast tightly covered in the refrigerator.

Tightly wrapped compressed yeast can be stored in the refrigerator and used by the expiration date printed on the package. It can also be frozen in a plastic bag for up to 3 months. (If compressed yeast gets moldy or discolors, you should throw it out.)

Substitutions

Quick-rising dry yeast can be substituted for active dry yeast.

One (.6 ounce) cake of compressed yeast = 1 (.25 ounce) packet of active dry yeast.

2 ½ teaspoons active dry yeast = 1 (.25 ounce) packet active dry yeast.

Usage

For best results, let your dough rise at a temperature between 70 to 85 degrees Fahrenheit.

When dissolving yeast in water, make sure the water temperature is between 105 and 115 degrees Fahrenheit. You want it warm enough to activate the yeast, but not hot enough to kill it.

You should also test, or "proof" your yeast before using it to be sure it's still active. To do this, dissolve the amount of yeast to be used in your recipe in the amount of warm water specified in the recipe and add a pinch of sugar. Set the mixture aside in a warm place for 5 to 10 minutes. If it starts to foam and expand, the yeast is alive and active.

Did you know? Each .25 ounce dry yeast envelope contains thousands of yeast cells.

FOOD	QUANTITY	YIELD
Almonds, sliced	2 ¼ oz.	½ cup
Almonds, slivered	2 oz.	⅓ cup
Apple pie filling	21 oz. can	2 ⅓ cups
Apples, fresh	1 medium	¾ cup chopped; 1 cup diced or sliced
Apples, fresh	1 lb.	3 medium; 2 ½ cups peeled, diced, or sliced; 3 cups unpeeled, diced, or sliced
Apple slices, canned	20 oz. can	2 drained
Apricots, canned	16 oz. can	2 cups drained halves; 6-8 whole
Apricots, dried	6 oz. pkg.	1 cup dried; 2 cups cooked
Apricots, fresh	2 medium	½ cup sliced
Apricots, fresh	1 lb.	2 cups halves or slices; 8-12 medium
Baking powder	7 oz. can	1 ¼ cups
Baking soda	16 oz. box	2 ⅓ cups
Bananas, dried, sliced	1 lb.	4–4 ½ cups
Bananas, fresh	1 medium	1 cup sliced

FOOD	QUANTITY	YIELD
Bananas, fresh	1 lb.	3 small or large; 1 ½ cups mashed; 2 cups sliced
Bisquick	60 oz. box	14 cups
Blueberries, canned	15 oz. can	1 ½ cups
Blueberries, fresh or frozen	1 lb.	3 ½ cups; makes 1 (9") pie
Blueberry pie filling	21 oz. can	2 ⅓ cups
Butter	2 tbsp.	"the size of a walnut"
Butter	¼ lb. stick	½ cup; 8 tbsp.; 12-16 pats; ⅓ cup clarified butter
Butter	½ lb.	25 servings
Butter	1 lb.	2 cups; 4 sticks
Butter, soft	8 oz. tub	1 cup
Butter, whipped	1 lb.	3 cups
Butterscotch morsels	12 oz. pkg.	2 cups
Cake mix	18.5 oz. box	5-6 cups batter; 2 (9" round) layers; 2 (8" square) layers; 1 (13" x 9" x 2") cake; 1 cartoon character cake; 24 cupcakes

FOOD	QUANTITY	YIELD
Cake, sheet (9" x 13")	1 ½ cakes	25 servings
Cake, two layer (9")	2–2 ½ cakes	25 servings
Cherries, canned, tart	16 oz. pitted	1 ½ cups drained
Cherries, dried, tart	3 oz. pkg.	½ cup
Cherries, fresh, sweet	1 lb. unpitted	1 quart; 1 ¾ cups
Cherries, frozen, tart	1 lb. pitted	2 cups
Cherry pie filling	21 oz. can	2 ⅓ cups
Chocolate, bar or square	1 oz.	3 tbsp. chopped or grated
Chocolate, bar or square	9 oz.	1 ⅝ cups chopped or grated; 1 cup
Melted Chocolate, unsweetened	1 oz.	1 square; 4 tbsp. grated
Chocolate, unsweetened	1 oz.	1 envelope liquid
Chocolate bits, M&M	12 oz. pkg	1 ½ cups
Chocolate kisses (mini)	10 oz. pkg.	209 pieces

FOOD	QUANTITY	YIELD
Chocolate morsels	12 oz. pkg.	2 cups
Chocolate wafers	20 wafers	1 cup fine crumbs
Cinnamon, ground	1 oz.	4 tbsp.
Cinnamon, stick	1" part of stick	1 tsp. ground
Cocoa, baking	8 oz. tin	2 ⅔ cups
Coconut, flaked	3 ½ oz. can	1 ¼ cups
Coconut, flaked	7 oz. pkg.	2 ½ cups
Coconut, flaked	14 oz. pkg.	5 ⅓ cups
Coconut, fresh	1 lb.	1 med.; 3 cups grated or chopped
Crackers, graham	15 (2 ½" sq.)	1 cup fine crumbs
Crackers, graham, crumbs	3 ¾ cups; 13 ½ oz. box	makes 3 pie shells
Cranberries, fresh	12 oz. pkg.	3 cups
Cranberries, fresh	1 lb. pkg.	4 cups; 3 cups cooked sauce
Cream, heavy	½ pint	1 cup unwhipped; 2 cups whipped
Cream, heavy (unwhipped)	¾ pint	25 servings

FOOD	QUANTITY	YIELD
Cream, Light (half-and-half)	1 pint	2 cups; 16 coffee servings
Cream, whipped, Pressurized	7 oz. can	1 ⅞ cups
Cream cheese	3 oz. pkg.	⅓ cup
Cream cheese	8 oz. pkg.	1 cup
Dates, diced,sugared	1 lb.	2 ⅔ cups
Dates, dried, pitted	8 oz. pkg.	54 dates; 1 ¼ cups chopped
Dates, dried, with pits	1 lb.	60 dates; 2 ½ cups pitted
Flour, all-purpose	5 lb. bag	20 cups sifted
Flour, cake	1 lb.	4 ⅛ cups unsifted; 4 ⅝ cups sifted
Flour, self-rising	1 lb.	4 cups sifted
Ginger, crystallized	1 tbsp.	1 tsp. ground
Ginger, fresh	1 tbsp. chopped	1 tsp. ground
Ginger, fresh	1 ½"-2" piece	2 tbsp. grated or chopped
Ginger, ground	½ tsp.	1 tsp. fresh chopped
Ginger, ground	1 oz.	4 tbsp.

FOOD	QUANTITY	YIELD
Lemons	1 lb.	4-6 medium; ⅔-1 cup juice
Macadamia nuts	7 oz. jar	1 ½ cups
Margarine	¼ lb. stick	½ cup; 8 tbsp.
Margarine	1 lb.	2 cups; 4 sticks
Margarine, soft	8 oz. tub	16 tbsp.
Marshmallow crème	7 oz. jar	2 ⅛ cups
Milk	1 quart	4 cups
Milk, sweetened, condensed	14 oz. can	1 ¼ cups
Mincemeat	27 oz. jar	2 ⅔ cups
Mincemeat, condensed	9 oz. box	½ cup
Molasses	12 oz. bottle	1 ½ cups
Oreo cookies	12 cookies	1 cup fine crumbs
Oreo cookies	1 lb., 4 oz. Pkg.	51 cookies
Peaches, canned, sliced	16 oz. can	2-2 ½ cups drained
Peaches, fresh	1 lb.	3-4 medium; 2 cups peeled and sliced or diced; 1 ½ cups pulp
Peaches, fresh	2 lbs.	makes 1 (9") pie

FOOD	QUANTITY	YIELD
Peaches, frozen	10 oz.	1 cup slices drained; 1 ¼ cups sliced with juice
Peach pie filling	21 oz. can	2 ⅓ cups
Pecans, chips or pieces	6 oz. pkg.	1 ½ cups
Raisins, seedless	1 lb. pkg.	3 cups
Raspberries, fresh	1 pint	1 ¾ cups
Raspberries, frozen	10 oz. pkg.	1 cup with syrup
Shortening, solid	1 lb. can	2 ½ cups
Shortening, sticks	20 oz. pkg.	3 sticks, 1 cup each
Strawberries, fresh	1 cup whole	4 oz.; ½ cup pureed
Strawberries, fresh	1 pint	2 ½ cups whole; 1 ¾ cups sliced; 1 ¼ cups pureed; 12 large, 24 medium or 36 small
Strawberries, frozen, sliced	10 oz. pkg.	1 cup drained; 1 ¼ cups with syrup
Strawberries, frozen, whole	20 oz. pkg.	4 cups whole; 2 ¼ cups pureed

FOOD	QUANTITY	YIELD
Strawberry pie filling	21 oz. can	2 ⅓ cups
Sugar, brown	1 lb.	2 ¼ cups packed
Sugar, confectioners	1 lb.	3 ¾ cups unsifted; 4 ¼ cups sifted
Sugar, granulated	1 lb.	2 ¼ cups
Sugar, granulated	5 lb. bag	11 ¼ cups
Sugar cubes	1 lb. box	96 cubes
Vanilla extract	1 oz.	2 ½ tbsp.
Vanilla wafers	30 wafers	1 cup fine crumbs
Walnuts, halves	7 oz. pkg.	1 ¾ cups
Walnuts, pieces	2 ½ oz. pkg.	½ cup
Whipped topping, frozen	8 oz. carton	3 ½ cups
Whipped topping mix	1.4 oz. pkg.	2 cups whipped topping

IF YOU NEED THIS	SUBSTITUTE THIS
2 tbsp. almonds, ground (for flavoring):	¼ tsp. almond extract
1 tsp. apple pie spice:	½ tsp. ground cinnamon+ ¼ tsp. ground nutmeg + ⅛ tsp. ground allspice + ⅛ tsp. ground cardamom
1 tsp. baking powder, double acting:	¼ tsp. baking soda + ½ cup buttermilk (Reduce other liquid in recipe by ½ cup)
2 ¾ cups biscuit mix:	2 cups flour, sifted with + 1 tbsp. baking powder 1 tsp. salt + ¼ cup shortening (cut in)
1 cup butter or margarine (for baking):	⅞ cup shortening + ½ tsp. salt
1 cup buttermilk:	1 tbsp. lemon juice or white vinegar + ⅞ cup + 1 tbsp. whole milk (let stand for 10 minutes)
1 cup buttermilk (for baking):	1 cup plain yogurt or 1 cup sour cream
6 oz. chocolate, morsels:	9 tbsp. cocoa powder + 7 tbsp. sugar + 3 tbsp. butter or margarine
2 oz. chocolate, semisweet:	⅓ cup chocolate chips
1 oz. chocolate, semisweet:	½ oz. unsweetened chocolate + 1 tbsp. sugar
1 oz. chocolate square, unsweetened:	3 ½ tbsp. cocoa powder + 2 tsp. butter or shortening

IF YOU NEED THIS	SUBSTITUTE THIS
1 cup coconut, grated:	1 ⅓ cups coconut, flaked
1 cup cream, heavy (for cooking, not whipping):	¾ cup whole milk + ⅓ cup butter
1 cup cream, light:	½ cup heavy cream + ½ cup whole milk
1 cup cream, light (for cooking):	⅞ cup whole milk + 3 tbsp. butter
1 cup cream, light (for cooking):	1 cup evaporated milk
1 cup cream, whipped sweetened:	4 oz. whipped topping
1 cup cream, whipped, sweetened:	1 ¼ oz. dessert topping mix, prepared
1 cup cream, whipping:	⅔ cup evaporated milk + 4 tsp. lemon juice or vinegar
1 cup cream, whipping:	½ cup nonfat dry milk + ⅓ cup water + 1 tbsp. lemon juice
1 tsp. cream of tartar:	1 tsp. lemon juice or vinegar
1 cup flour, cake, sifted:	⅞ cup all purpose flour + 2 tbsp. cornstarch
1 cup flour, self-rising sifted:	1 cup all purpose flour + 1 ½ tsp. baking powder + ¼ tsp. salt (Mix and substitute measure for measure for self rising flour. Omit any additional baking powder and/or salt called for in recipe.)
1 ½ cups fruit, fresh, cut up:	16 oz. canned fruit, drained

IF YOU NEED THIS	SUBSTITUTE THIS
1 ¼ cups fruit, fresh, cut up:	10 oz. frozen fruit, drained
1 cup half and half:	⅞ cup whole milk + 1 ½ tsp. butter
1 cup half and half:	½ cup light cream + ½ cup whole milk
1 tsp. lemon or lime peel, fresh:	1 tsp. lemon or lime peel, dried
1 tsp. lemon or lime peel, fresh (for flavoring):	½ tsp. lemon or lime extract
1 cup milk, condensed (sweetened):	1 cup nonfat dry milk + ½ cup boiling water . + ⅔ cup sugar + 3 tbsp. melted butter (Process mixture in blender until smooth)
1 cup milk, evaporated:	1 cup cream
1 cup milk, whole:	½ cup evaporated milk + ½ cup water
8 cups pie crust mix:	6 ¼ cups flour, mixed with + 1 tbsp. salt + 2 ½ cups shortening (cut in)
1 cup sour cream (for baking):	¾ cup sour milk or buttermilk + ⅓ cup butter
1 cup sour cream (for baking):	1 cup plain yogurt + 1 tsp. baking soda

OVEN TEMPERATURES

Fahrenheit	Description	Celsius
200°	Very cool	95°
225°	Cool	110°
250°	Very slow	120°
300°	Slow	150°
325°	Warm	165°
350°	Moderate	175°
375°	Moderately hot	190°
400°	Hot	200°
450°	Very hot	230°
500°	Extremely hot	260°

INDEX

Lemon Cake 50
Lemon Cream Cheese
  Swirl Cake 30
Pear Caramel Ribbon Cake 38
Pineapple Upside Down Cake 53
Ricotta Raisin Cake 48
Self-Frosting
  Mexican Chocolate Cake 54
Strawberry Lemon Cake with
  Fluffy Cream Cheese Frosting 32

SOUR CREAM
Apricot Brandy Cake 70
Brownie Bottom Cheesecake 209
Cinnamon Bun Cake 35
Cookies and Cream Layer Cake 114
Cream Cheese Filled Coffee
  Cake Rolls 142
Date Spice Cake
  with Brown Sugar Glaze 85
Ginger Cake 100
Iced Lemon Poppy Seed
  Cookies 172
Lemon Cake 50
Lemon Cheesecake Bars with
  White Chocolate Frosting 222
Mocha S'Mores Pie 239
Orange Banana Bundt Cake
  with Buttermilk Glaze 95
Orange Walnut Coffee Cake 86
Raspberry Sour Cream Cake 97
Spicy Apple Tart 251
Strawberry Bundt Cake 94
Turtle Pie 243
Two-Toned Chocolate
  Cheesecake 252

SPECIAL CAKES
Chocolate Filled Cupcakes 137
Cinnamon Rolls 140
Colossal Petit Fours 138
Cream Cheese Filled
  Coffee Cake Rolls 142
Sticky Buns 144

SPECIAL COOKIES
Chocolate Turtle Cookies 186
Chocolate-Dipped
  Malted Milk Cookies 194
Gingerbread Rolled Cookies 190
Orange Chocolate Filled
  Cookies 192
Spicy Cinnamon Twists 188

SPECIAL TOUCHES
Candied Pecans 16
Chocolate Leaves 17

Colored Sugar 16

SPECIAL TREATS
Banana Chocolate Treat 254
Pistachio Marshmallow Salad 255
Spicy Apple Tart 251
Two-Toned Chocolate
  Cheesecake 252

SPICE CAKE MIX
Autumn Spice Cake 108
Date Spice Cake
  with Brown Sugar Glaze 85
Gingerbread Rolled Cookies 190
Oatmeal Raisin Cookies 157
Oatmeal Spice Cake
  with Brown Sugar Frosting 104
Pear Caramel Ribbon Cake 38
Spicy Apple Tart 251
Spicy Walnut Rum Cake 66
Zucchini Cake with Lemon
  Cream Cheese Frosting 112
Spicy Apple Tart 251
Spicy Cinnamon Twists 188
Spicy Oatmeal Cookies 167
Spicy Walnut Rum Cake 66
Sticky Buns 144

STRAWBERRIES
Banana Split Torte 124
Cool and Fruity Lemon Cake 24
Ginger Jam Sandwich Cookies 180
Honey-Nut Oatmeal Jam Bars 215
Strawberry Banana Cake 96
Strawberry Bundt Cake 94
Strawberry Cream Cheese Bars 218
Strawberry Lemon Cake with
  Fluffy Cream Cheese Frosting 32
Strawberry Banana Cake 96
Strawberry Bundt Cake 94
Strawberry Cream Cheese Bars 218
Strawberry Lemon Cake with
  Fluffy Cream Cheese Frosting 32

SUGAR COOKIE MIX
Basic Thumbprint Cookie
  Recipe 151
Black Forest Cherry Cookies 174
Cherry Cheesecake Bars 224
Chocolate Pecan Pie Squares 198
Chocolate Pinwheels 178
Chocolate-Dipped Malted
  Milk Cookies 194
Cream Cheese Apricot Cookies 156
Date Nut Pinwheel Cookies 177
Ginger Jam Sandwich Cookies 180

Watergate Cake 88
Watermelon Cake
   with Lime Frosting 119
White Chocolate Bundt Cake 80
White Chocolate Macadamia Nut
   Cookies 162

WHITE CHOCOLATE
Cherry Cake 118
Colossal Petit Fours 138
Lemon Cheesecake Bars with
   White Chocolate Frosting 222
Never-Ending Chocolate
   Bundt Cake 78
White Chocolate Bundt Cake 80
White Chocolate Bundt Cake 80
White Chocolate Macadamia Nut
   Cookies 162

Y
YELLOW CAKE MIX
Apple Cider Bundt Cake 89
Apple Cranberry Streusel 40
Apple Crumb Cake 45
Apple Date Coffe Cake 92
Applesauce Cake
   with Paraline Topping 21
Apricot Brandy Cake 70
Apricot Oatmeal Bars 217
Apricot Streusel Bundt Cake 74
Banana Chocolate Treat 254
Banana Layer Cake
   with Butter Pecan Frosting 110
Banana Nut Cake 33
Blueberry Cream Cheese Cake 77
Blueberry Crunch 249
Cinnamon Rolls 140
Cool and Fruity Lemon Cake 24
Cream Cheese Filled
   Coffee Cake Rolls 142
Fluffy Orange Cake 22
Lemon Raspberry Crumb Bars 200
Luscious Orange Torte 122
Marbled Cheesecake Bars 223
Orange Banana Bundt Cake
   with Buttermilk Glaze 95
Orange Meringue Torte
   with Apricot Filling 134
Orange -Topped Lemon
   Bundt Cake 76
Orange Walnut Coffee Cake 86
Pecan Pie Bars 202
Pineapple Rum Cake 60
Sticky Buns 144
Two-Toned Chocolate
   Cheesecake 252

Z
Zucchini Cake with Lemon
   Cream Cheese Frosting 112

307

My Personal Index

Page #	Recipe Name	Comments

My Personal Index

Page #	Recipe Name	Comments

My Personal Index

Page #	Recipe Name	Comments

My Personal Index

Page #	Recipe Name	Comments

My Personal Index

Page #	Recipe Name	Comments

My Personal Index

Page #	Recipe Name	Comments

My Personal Index

Page #	Recipe Name	Comments

My Personal Index

Page #	Recipe Name	Comments

COOKBOOKS PUBLISHED BY COOKBOOK RESOURCES

Mother's Recipes

•

Recipe Keepsakes

•

Kitchen Keepsakes & More Kitchen Keepsakes

•

Quick Fixes With Mixes

•

Cooking With 5 Ingredients Cookbook

•

The New Cooking With 4 Ingredients Cookbook

•

Mealtimes and Memories

•

Cookbook 25 Years

•

Texas Longhorn Cookbook

•

Little Taste of Texas I

•

Little Taste of Texas II

•

Leaving Home

•

Cookin' With Will Rogers

•

Best of Busy People's Cookbook

•

Homecoming

•

Best of Lone Star Legacy

•

Simply Simpatico

•

Pass The Plate

*

The Authorized Texas Ranger Cookbook